# You'll Never Be Loved
## |Breaking the Labels|

*He loves you!*
*♡ Anna S.*

ANNA STAMPER

Foreword by KIM KIMBERLING, PhD

*Cover by:* © *Anna Stamper*

*Cover Photo by:* © *Caleb Collins Photography*

*Back Cover Photo by:* © *Caleb Collins Photography*

This book contains stories in which the author has changed people's names in order to preserve their privacy.

*Father God,*

*I come to You today as I begin writing this book. You know that, for the last couple years, I have been too scared to try this, even though I have felt Your prompting many times.*

*Today I am putting down the fear of failing and I am going to have faith and confidence that You will lead me through this.*

*Please guide my hand and mind as I strive to honor You with this book. Give me the strength to be open and share when it is hard. Give me the hope to pass on to someone who needs hope. Give me the wisdom to say what needs to be said and also the wisdom to know when to be silent. Give me the insight to what You would have me to share. Speak through me, shine through me, let others see You through me. Let me be a tool for You.*

*Give me peace and comfort during the sleepless nights and protect my heart when I have bad dreams from going back through all of this again. Please, God, walk by my side.*

*You know the fears I have of writing my story. I pray that if Dad and Mom see this book their eyes and their hearts will be open. I pray it will not put more of a wedge in our relationship. I only want this to bring good to people's lives. You know the intent of my heart and I am trusting You.*

*God, I give You full control over this book. Lead it where You would have it to go.*

# CONTENTS

Forward By Kim Kimberling, PhD

A Note to My Readers     1

1   No One Will Ever Love Me     3

2   Sorry Is Not Enough     13

3   Burning Bridges     21

4   Honor Thy Father and Thy Mother     31

5   You Are a World Changer     41

6   Trust     51

7   We All Have a Special Calling     59

8   You Hurt Because You Love     69

9   Fear     79

10   Will I Ever Have a Real Relationship?     89

11   My Real Family     101

# FOREWORD BY KIM KIMBERLING, PHD

As a counselor, I often see people who believe a lie as truth. Actually, I think all of us could fit into that category at least once in our lifetimes. Many of these "lies" we do not remember; or they were fairly harmless, so they did not stick. Some may have been said by peers as we grew up and some by those in authority over us. The more significant the person was to us, the higher the probability that we would actually believe the lie. A negative comment about a seven-year-old's weight, for example, might have less of an impact coming from a peer than from a parent or teacher. To believe a lie as truth, there has to be this perfect combination of how we feel about ourselves when it is said and the significance of our relationship to the person who said it. Some of the lies just bounce off us like water on a duck's back, but some stick and become a template that we lay over our lives. These are the deadly ones that can impact us from the moment someone says them to us until the end of our lives.

What if someone you trusted told you that "no one will ever love you"? What if that someone was your pastor? That is what happened to Anna Stamper, and with her life experiences she believed this lie to be true. *You'll Never Be Loved* is a powerful book. Like me, you may find yourself wishing parts of this book were fiction because of the incomprehensible gravity of the pain that life's circumstances brought Anna. Yet, this book is more than just a story about Anna. It is a story we can all relate to at some level because each of us has been hurt by someone else. As Anna tells her story, she gives her readers many opportunities to stop and deal with their own stories. She also shares meaningful Scripture verses that speak God's truth over lies.

*You'll Never Be Loved* is in essence a love story. It is one each of us needs to hear and one each of us can embrace because we have a God who loves us enough to erase all the lies we have ever believed. So find a quiet place, get out your pen, and prepare to be transformed as God uses Anna's story to change your life.

## Kim Kimberling, PhD
Founder of the Awesome Marriage Movement
Author of *7 Secrets to an Awesome Marriage*

Anna Stamper

# A NOTE TO MY READERS

First of all, thank you for taking a moment to read my book.

I wrote this book because I have a story to tell, and I want my story to strengthen someone.

I was raised in central Oklahoma, out in the country. I was raised in a very conservative Christian home, homeschooled, and very sheltered.

I was raised believing I was not worth anything and no one loved me, or ever would. I was led to believe that no one wanted any type of relationship with me, and I was a waste of space.

Once I got out of that environment in my mid-twenties, I learned the truth about what God really says about me. God loves me so much that He would send His only son to die for me, even if I was the only one on earth. He loves me so much that He wants a personal relationship with me.

My life had changed so much since I left that unhealthy environment, and I finally realize that I am God's special child. I want to share that hope with someone.

It has not been easy going back through everything in my past, but if I can give hope to only one person, it will be more than worth it.

By writing this book, I want to give someone hope that no matter what anyone has told them, God loves them so much. I want to give someone hope that they are truly worth something, and they have a special calling of their own.

God has a plan for each of us and no one else can fulfill that plan for us.

I cannot even explain how much I have prayed through this project. I have prayed, lying in bed crying because I was wakened by bad dreams over and over. I have prayed, crying with joy, because of the amazing things God has taught me. I have prayed as I read my journals over for the first time since I was a child, at times, weeping for that sad, scared, broken child. I have lain awake, praying for this book that I would have the words to finish it. I have prayed for those who will be reading this book, that it would impact their lives.

While writing this book, I have grown even closer to God as I have relied on Him for strength and wisdom and guidance. Over and over again, He shows me just how much He cares for me and wants the very best for me. I pray that God will touch your life as much as He has touched mine, and you will come to realize just how special you are. I pray that you will come to understand that you are one of God's special treasures, regardless what anyone has ever said about you.

You can break the labels that people have placed on you.

If you would like to share your own personal story, or share how this book has impacted your life, I would love to hear from you!

neverloved.book@gmail.com

www.facebook.com/Youll-Never-Be-Loved-958221214259766

# ONE

## NO ONE WILL EVER LOVE ME

"Will I ever matter to anyone?" "Will anyone ever love me?"
I asked myself these questions many, many times in the first 15 years of my life. It was about that time when, in my mind, the question became a statement.
I will never matter to anyone. No one will ever love me. Period. No question about it.

As a teenager, I felt that the times I tried to be my true self were those in which I suffered the most ridicule.
When I spent time with other teens in our church group, I often tried to enter into the conversation and they would make jokes about my comments and tell me to play the "quiet mouse" game... by myself.
When I was silent, I was teased about being quiet and awkward.
I did not know how to make everyone accept me, but I knew, beyond a shadow of a doubt, that just being myself was not the answer.
Growing up, I was never close to my dad. Really, none of us kids were close to either parent, but certain personalities allowed Dad to relate to some better than others.
Some were tough and would just fight back, and others were more emotional... yep, you guessed it... I am the latter, and my dad never knew how to handle emotional people.
As I have gotten older, I have grown to understand more and more that Dad was not trained to respond to emotions and, in turn, never knew how

3

to deal with emotions in his children.

The answer was always "Get tough!" and "Take it like a man!" For the record, I was not created with the ability to "take it like a man."

The chasm between Dad's "get tough" methods and my "you just broke my heart" personality brought a lot of pain in my life.

Struggles were everywhere: working for him, years of piano lessons, and just everyday life. All of it eventually led me to attend a church that Dad didn't approve of.

It always left an empty place in my life and hurt me deeply, the feeling that Dad "loved" all of my siblings and didn't love me.

I understand now that what I saw then as "loving" them was actually that he could just relate with them better than he could relate to me.

I was the child who had the big imagination, and I journaled about everything. I took my journal and walked as far from the house as I could. I would sit on an outcrop of rocks, overlooking my Grandpa's old runway. I would write, and dream, and pretend I was all alone. It was easier to pretend than deal with the reality that I was in the middle of a family that didn't even love me.

*"...I wonder what it would feel like to know that your dad and mom love you? I wonder if I will ever know how it feels? Will I ever know how it feels to have anyone love me, or want me?..." -journal entry (age 12)*

Sitting in the cow pasture, out by Grandpa's old hanger, I would wonder what would happen if I never went back home.

Would anyone come looking for me?

Would anyone even notice that I was gone?

With all of my heart, I believed that no one wanted me around, much less actually loved me.

I wasn't accepted by other teenagers at church, whether I was talking or silent. I was of no use to Dad because I couldn't work as hard as a full-grown man, even though I tried my very hardest. I was a failed void filler for Dad and Mom. They had only gotten pregnant with me because my sister, Katie, born a year before me with a heart defect, had only lived for 11 days. Dad and Mom were sad so they got pregnant with another baby to fill that void in their lives. Once they realized I could not replace Katie, they really didn't want me. Yes, I truly believed this until about two and a half years ago when God began to show me, through a series of events, a whole new meaning for my life. He started showing me that, just maybe, I was worth something.

When I was about sixteen years old, I was really hurting because Dad didn't even pretend to want me. I turned to the next person that would break my heart, the minister of the church that I was raised in.

Richard had a daughter my age, and they had the "perfect" father-daughter relationship. I thought surely he could help me figure out how to make Dad want me.

I should take a moment here and share a little about the "church" that I grew up in.

It is a non-denominational group of about 60-80 Christians who do not want to be called a "church" because that makes them sound like the "rest of the world", instead, we were the "assembly".

It is a very conservative, confused, and controlled-by-men group of Christians with an entire network of groups throughout the US, Mexico, Peru, and Canada, and we had "meetings" instead of "services."

The "ministers" are men deemed qualified, by other men, to make and enforce rules and regulations as they see fit.

An example of these rules and regulations are that women are not allowed to cut their hair, wear makeup, earrings, or pants. All women must wear skirts that are well below the knees at all times.

Women are very demeaned and looked down upon. Women do not work outside of the home, nor do they have an education past a high school diploma. They often get married at a very young age, and start their family soon after.

In this group, women are very smothered and suppressed; they are molded into what the ministers want them to become, never what God created them to be.

When I started talking to Richard, what I knew was that, as a minister, his way was the right way, no questions asked.

I had no idea that I was signing up for seven years of frustration, hurt, and emotional abuse.

Every time I would talk to Richard about something that was happening in my teenage world, the answer would always come back to,

"Well, because of your home life, you will always be insecure."

That would be like telling a child, "Because your dad only had one leg, you will never walk correctly."

It has taken me many years to understand that the things Richard told me, and I believed about myself, were emotional abuse.

Richard never physically harmed me, but even more dangerously, I believed that my life was not worth the air I breathed. I believed everyone's lives would be so much better if I was not in theirs at all, and there was a period of time when I tried to find the courage to make everyone's lives better.

"God, why did you let me be born if the whole world would be better without me?

Why did You let Katie die if they actually wanted her? You could have let her live and taken me.

God, I can't live for another 50-60 years with no one ever loving me.

I can't do it! Please take me now."

This is the prayer I prayed over and over, so many times as I walked out to the far cow pasture, weeping until I was sick, sometimes I would fall asleep on the rocks. Most days I would stay out there until well after dark. Sometimes I would ride my horse, Stormy, for several hours just to get away from home, or spend hours at the barn playing with the horse because that was one place where I felt safe.

I faced the question of, will I ever be loved or wanted for several years as a child and teen.

Then one day in 2005, when I was 19 years old, Richard spoke 6 words that would answer that question for me; 6 words no one should ever be told.

"No one will ever love you".

And the worst part of it is that I believed him. I never even questioned this statement. He was the minister so what he says is truth, right?

That day he told me, "No one will ever love; no one will ever want someone like you." I didn't know what to do with that. I didn't know how to process what I had been told. At that point in my life, I didn't really even know how to recognize the feelings that I felt.

I really wasn't upset by what Richard had told me; I just accepted it as truth and knew I would just have to learn how to make it through the rest of my life alone. I knew I would be on my own forever.

Has anyone ever told you something that took away all hope? I promise you, that is not what God says about your life!

_____

_____

_____

_____

_____

_____

For the 6 years following my talks with Richard about no one ever wanting me, I lived a very sad and depressing life. I went from day to day knowing I would never be married or have a family of my own.

I had been doing very well at my job at the bank, moving from teller to new accounts, eventually managing a branch, and even being awarded the Employee of the Year. Even still, I knew it would never matter in the long run because I was only working outside of the home because I was a screw-up and no man would want to marry me. I believed I would never have the chance to be a wife or a mother, and it broke my heart.

And much like I did as a child, I would go home after work, lie on the floor and cry until I had made myself sick; crying out to God, asking Him, "Why did You put me on this earth if I was going to be all alone? Why couldn't I just die and be done with all of this pain? If the only thing a woman can do is get married and have kids, it was obvious I was not going to ever have that chance, so why did I have to live and be miserable for the rest of my life?"

Then on November 4th, 2012, three years ago almost to the day, God sent me on a crazy awesome journey that I am still on.

This journey began when Rachel, a friend from work, kept pestering me about going to church with her. I kept refusing to go with her, over and over, knowing I couldn't ever go to a different church. One thing I need to mention about the church I grew up in is that they believe that they are the only "right Christians." One of the "rules" is that you must only attend one of their groups, or you are going against God's will, leading you to be "marked", which is their way of shunning someone, of course, disguised as "tough love." So, of course, I could not go to church with this girl from work.

Finally, after being asked over and over, I made a deal with Rachel that if I went to her church one time, she would stop asking me. She agreed and we planned to go to her church on a Saturday night so that I could go to my normal church on Sunday. No one would be the wiser.

I attended Life.Church, at the OKC Campus, for the first time in early November of 2012, and I was a little overwhelmed, to be very honest.

I had been raised with only the piano and a hymnal for worship. When all the spotlights came on, and a guy came out in skinny jeans and earrings and started dancing around the stage while he sang and played the guitar, I was a little freaked out.

I stood there, in the center of the front row, wearing my long denim skirt, and praying that God would not strike me with lightning right then and there.

I knew if anyone ever found out about this, I would be "marked" on the spot.

I would be sent away from the group and no one, including my family, would ever be allowed to speak with me again. Little did I know I would willingly walk away later on.

I finally made it through worship, which ended with a video promo of the message series. I will never forget that video clip; it was of a woman washing dishes in a kitchen sink. The woman filled the sink with water and added soap and then, while she was washing a dish, the water turned to blood, and then she dropped the dish on the floor and Revelations 11:6 scrolled across the screen. Another thing I will never forget was a 7' red moon hanging from the ceiling of the stage.

I was so nervous. These were some really strange people, and they had really weird ways.

The next day, Sunday, I went to the meeting hall for "normal" church with my family. I felt like everyone could tell I had done something bad the evening before. I knew someone would be able to tell I had sinned by attending a different church and I would be cast out on the spot.

But no one found out… for 6 very long months.

After that first night at Life.Church, I didn't go back for a few weeks because that stuff about the rapture made me pretty nervous. My friend from work asked me to go back again for a different message series because she realized it probably hadn't been the best time to take someone new to church, so I decided I would go back again and give it another chance.

*"…Saturday night, Rachel and I went to Life.Church. I know I shouldn't be going there but I really like it and I feel like I get so much more out of it than I do at meeting…"* - *journal entry Dec 24, 2012*

The more I attended Life.Church and as I started building relationships there, the more I began to understand and learn about God's love for me.

I started to understand more and more about how wrong Richard had been all those years.

Don't get me wrong, none of these things happened overnight, and I am still learning so much each day, but I started processing and thinking about all of the things I had believed all of my life.

I finally began to understand God loves me because I am HIS child.

He wants me to have an amazing life because I am HIS child.

One day I was in the shower praying to God and just thanking Him for where He was taking me and for all the things He was showing me, when I had an epiphany… God didn't let me be born so I could finish Katie's journey, since she died at such a young age.

God knew she would only be on this earth for 11 days and that is all He had planned for her. He did not plan a long healthy life for her and then was taken by surprise when she got sick. He knew she would only live for 11 days, and that I would be born a year later.

God knew I would have a different personality than the rest of my siblings.

God knew I would struggle with feeling unloved and unwanted, but He used that situation so I could become who I am now.

God knew from the very beginning that if I continued to call out to Him in my pain and hurt, He could mold that into something beautiful.

Yes, I am still single, and I do not know if that will change, but that doesn't mean no one loves me; or no one wants me.

I REFUSE to believe that lie any longer!

MY GOD loves me and wants me. And that is so much more precious than any man, any father, any mother, any minister, or any other person wanting me or loving.

*"For we are God's masterpiece. He has created us anew in Christ Jesus, so we can do the good things He planned for us long ago"* Ephesians 2:10

What have you been made to believe about yourself? Have you ever done something you think is "too big" or "too bad" to forgive?

_____

_____

_____

_____

_____

_____

Let me tell you this- God still loves you more than you can even imagine! Even when we hurt Him or disappoint Him, He is still there with His arms open for us.

He is always there for us. Waiting for us to turn to Him.

Has someone ever told you that you are worthless? Have you ever had your heart broken over and over?

God is there to heal us.

Often times we try so hard to always "have it all together" and not need anyone's help, but that is our pride acting out. God wants to be there for us, to put us back together, but we are often too proud to let Him.

I try to always remember the truth that the Apostle Paul wrote to the Romans

*"If God is for us, who can ever be against us?" Romans 8:31*

If my God says I am worthy and loved, then who dare say I will never be loved?
If my God has chosen me to be His child, than who dare say otherwise?

I have chosen that no man shall ever again have the power over me to make me believe that God does not love me and does not want me. God made me just how He wanted me.
He made me perfect for the plan He has chosen for me, and my joy is at its fullest when I let go of my hurt and let Him lead me wherever He wants me to go.

One of the things that helped me let go of the hurt Richard caused in my life, with his poisonous words, was to deal with them and recognize them for what they are, lies.

I would encourage you to sit down with your Bible and pray for God to guide you to truths that would help you understand what you are to Him.
Ask God to help you face your hurts, and then to leave them with Him.
If it helps, write down a list of truths you find about what God says about you. Paste it on your mirror or your fridge; somewhere you will see it every day.
A while back, I also took some quiet time and wrote down a list of all the people who are in my life and I know beyond a doubt they love me for who I am. This may sound prideful to some, but it can be done in a humble spirit, and I believe it was a very healthy exercise. It helped me to have a tangible object in my hands that reminded me I am a very loved and blessed person.
It was also a reminder that I am not who Richard labeled me as.
I chose to be who God labeled me as… a sheep in His pasture.
A Child of The King!

*"Even before He made the world, God loved us and chose us in Christ to be holy and without fault in His eyes" Ephesians 1:4*

Notes:

_____

_____

_____

_____

_____

_____

_____

_____

_____

_____

_____

_____

_____

_____

_____

_____

_____

Father God, tonight I pray Your peace and comfort over anyone who is facing the labels they have been given by other people or themselves. Help them to be open and honest about the hurts that are in their lives and scarred into their heart.

Father, I pray these people who have been hurt by human kind can come to understand how much You truly love them, and desire a very intimate relationship with them.

I pray they will feel Your presence!

Anna Stamper

# TWO

## SORRY IS NOT ENOUGH

This chapter is very sad for me to write as it was a very painful time in my life. As I mentioned earlier, I was about 16 years old when Richard stepped into my life as a father-figure.

Richard has known our family since long before I was born, and I spent a lot of time over at their house as they have a daughter, Julia, who is very close to my age.

I was always jealous of the "perfect" relationship Julia had with her dad. I always hoped someday my dad would realize how badly I wanted him to love me.

But he never did and Richard started filling that hole in my life.

When I needed to talk, he was there and would listen. When I was struggling through high school on my own, he was there to spend hours on the back deck helping me figure it out. When I thought a boy was cute, he was there to keep me practical. When I got a job, he was there to go car shopping with me.

He was there as a father to me for most of my teen years and even into my twenties. I really did value his input in my life because I felt like someone finally cared about me enough to be invested in my life. I didn't know then that the influence he was pouring into my life was not a healthy influence, and I would be dealing with pieces of the results for the rest of my life. I didn't know that for many years, just speaking his name would make me have bad, vivid dreams in which I was drowning or suffocating. I didn't know that just thinking about him would make me go back into the shell I had finally learned to come out of.

I didn't know those things then, but I have to always remember that I also wouldn't be the person I am today if it had not been for me having to learn to trust again and in doing that, learned in Whom to place my trust.

*"But when I am afraid, I will put my trust in You"*     *Psalm 56:3*

*"...my turkey day was not that fun. Laney and her family were here and she totally threw me under the bus to Richard about something that I had confided in her and Richard is freaking out on me today. What is the point in having a best friend if I can't confide in her when I need to just vent about things?..."*

           *-journal entry November 26, 2009*

In November of 2009, when I was 22 years old, I had a falling out with a really close friend of mine because of a "he-said-she-said" situation where Julia got her feelings hurt and Richard came down on me like a ton of bricks.

At the time I had no idea anything was wrong; I had said too much to the wrong person and they went to someone else and so on.

When it was brought to my attention that I had said too much, I went to the people involved and apologized. I thought the problem was taken care of and that life would go on. I had seen my wrong and had done what I knew to correct it, but Richard was not so quick to forgive and forget.

Richard drug the situation out for months and every time he had the chance to bring it up again, he did.

At least once a week he would make me go upstairs at the meeting hall and we would talk about it again. Every single time we would go over it, I came away feeling like a terrible person, and that there was no point to living life if I was such a bad person.

I never thought about the fact that maybe Richard was wrong or maybe I should get someone else's view of the situation-facts are facts and I was a loser.

I remember there were several times on a Sunday evening or Wednesday night after meeting that I would come downstairs after talking to Richard about the situation again, and literally be sick from being so upset about this. Other people would see that I had been crying, but I couldn't talk to them about it because Richard had told me that this situation needed to stay between him and I and that I was not allowed to talk to anyone else about it.

I am, by nature, a chatty person, but because I was teased so much as a teenager about talking too much, and then with other situations where Richard and my parents always said I was lying, I got to where I really wouldn't talk much at all. I became a wall flower and wouldn't enter into group activities or anything where the focus would be on me. This situation caused me to be even quieter. I was living in fear. I knew that talking had gotten me into this mess, and I wasn't allowed to talk to anyone about it. But it was so upsetting that I was really afraid that I was just going to explode one day and tell everyone what a terrible person I was.

I would dread even going to meeting because I knew that if Richard got a few minutes, he would make me go back upstairs and talk about all that I had done wrong again and again, and I didn't know how much more I could take, but Richard was the *minister* so he had to be right.

One Sunday night, Richard and I were upstairs and he was once again going over how I had to show that I was truly sorry for what I had done, and I told him that I had asked those that I had hurt to forgive me. I had asked God to forgive me, and I had tried really, really hard to change my ways so that I wouldn't ever make that mistake again. I didn't know what else to do. I told him that I was as sorry as I knew how to be. Richard turned and looked at me and said, "Anna, sorry is not enough", and then he walked away.

At that moment, I hurt so deeply I didn't know what to do. I knew that I was a horrible person, and I didn't know how to fix it. I didn't know how to be any sorrier for what I had done, and I knew that if I didn't even know how to be sorry enough, I would never be a good person.

And if sorry was not enough, I didn't know what else to do.

I sat upstairs, sobbing, not knowing what to do next. I knew that I could not go downstairs and act like everything was okay, but I also knew that I couldn't sit upstairs forever.

I thought maybe I should just start walking home and maybe I would get hit by a car, or maybe some stranger would pick me up and take me away. I just knew that if I was such a horrible person and if I had disappointed Richard that badly, there was no point in life.

If Richard was that disappointed in me, than God had probably totally given up on me, and He, for sure, would never love me.

I laid in bed for hours that night, trying to think of a way that I could just disappear. It was too hard to live in a world where no one loved me and where I made everyone else's life harder, but it made me even sadder to realize that even if I did end my life, no one would even care.

For the next year or so, I often tried to think of ways to end my life. I worked with Dad a lot, operating large equipment and there were so many times when I wanted to just pop it into gear and get in front of it so that it would just run over me and everyone would be happier. It was a very dark time for me.

*"...I don't think Richard is ever going to forgive me for the things I said to Laney. I can't even write about all that has happened the last couple months. It hurts too badly. Why did God even let me be born if no one wants me here? I don't understand..."*
*-journal entry December 2009*

I let this situation hang over my head for the next 4-5 years, believing that I was a failure and that I would never be forgiven.

The friend, with whom I had the falling out originally, and I never became friends again. I was sure that her parents would never want me around because I was a bad person, and there were even some young girls that I was cautioned to not spend one on one time with because I could be a bad influence on them.

Finally, there was another situation with some other young people in the assembly where someone had "messed up" and Richard rebuked those involved, from the stage in front of the entire congregation, about being repentant, and being sorry.

I remember sitting there and feeling very uncomfortable but not really being able to figure why. Then it hit me.

Because "sorry is not enough".

I had pulled back even more since I was told those words, and I did not rely on Richard as much as before because I knew that I was a hopeless cause. I was only a disappointment to him. When I started feeling very uneasy with how the current situation was being handled, I started paying closer attention, and I realized that the other young people were going through the same thing that I had faced all those years ago.

I can remember, very vividly, the first time I ever told anyone about what Richard had told me about not being sorry.

I had a couple from church over for dinner at my little tiny house and they had asked me a question about Richard. For the first time ever, I told them about the situation that I had faced a few years before. I was very embarrassed because I still believed that I was at fault and I hated to admit to these friends what a terrible person I was. My friend's reaction totally blew me away. Anger, and it was not directed at me. Anger at what Richard had led me to believe. I tried to make my friend understand that it wasn't Richard's fault but mine. I had done wrong, I was the bad person.

But after that conversation, I started to question things. Had Richard handled that situation right? Was I really totally at fault?

I didn't know these answers, but the questions were there, and I believe that it was God's way of planting a seed that would one day, far down the road, be watered and brought to light.

To this day, I struggle at times, when I feel like I have messed up, and I feel like I am never going to be a good person. There are times when I feel like God is going to give up on me because I just can't seem to "get it together."

But that is not how God works! God already approves of us and wants the best for us. We have to live our life knowing, with strong confidence, that God loves us *already* and no matter what we do, that will never change.

Yes, I know that I have not been, and never will be, perfect, but God forgives me when I sin, and I can keep going. It is not a man's place to tell me that I am not forgiven for something that I did not do against him. God knows my heart, and I believe that He fully forgave me for anything that I did wrong to hurt my friend's feelings all those years ago. I do not have to prove to a human that I was "sorry enough."

*"He has removed our sins as far from us as the east is from the west"*     *Psalm 103:12*

I never wrote about this situation in my journal. This is really saying something because I write about *everything.* But I was so ashamed and just wanted to forget the whole thing. I hoped that, by not writing about it, no one would have to know about it if I decided that I was going to just end my life.

It makes me very sad now to think of the relationships that have been lost because of one man's opinion and judgment.

There was another time that I faced a similar situation, a few years earlier, in December of 2005, when I was 18 years old, a young guy came from another area  to Oklahoma to work with Richard for several months and learn more about the house building trade. While this young man was in town, we spent a lot of time together, at Richard's house, meetings, gatherings and such.

We really hit it off well and were great friends by the end of his time here. I knew that he was interested in one of my closest friends who lived in another state, but I also knew that she did not like him, but had told him that she would give him a yes or no next time he came back through the area. I had really grown to like this guy since we had spent so much time together.

When it was time for him to leave, I told him that if this other girl didn't want to date him when he got back to her area, that he should come back here because I liked him.

Yeah, a little bold, I know, but not an unforgivable sin.

The guy that I was talking to told Richard what I had said and then Richard came to me about it and was very angry.

He talked to me about how dishonorable it was that I had been that forward with a guy. He went on to tell me that I was acting like a desperate and wanton woman, and that no man wants a woman who is like that.

He quoted me the story in John 8 about the woman who was caught in adultery. He told me that there are women, all over the world, that throw themselves at men and that is where I will end up if I acted this way.

I felt so terrible and dirty, and I knew that if anyone ever found out about this that I would be ruined forever. No one would ever want to marry me.

Richard told me that we would never tell anyone about this as it would be devastating to this guy's future wife and my future husband. I carried that burden around for nearly 10 years before I finally had the courage to tell someone about it.

As I write about this now, I am filled with a righteous anger at how I was made to feel about myself. I didn't do anything wrong with this guy; I merely told him that I liked him, but yet I, as a young girl, was made to feel as if I had ruined myself forever.

I can remember being so devastated over this and knowing that I couldn't tell anyone. Even years later, attending this guy's wedding as he married one of my friends and later visiting them at their home, I felt like such a bad person. I felt like I was cheating by not telling my friend, his wife, what I had told him.

I am so thankful now that I can live without guilt of both of these situations.

Not only was I not nearly as guilty as I was made to feel, but also, where I was wrong, God forgave me for all of my sins!

God does not beat us down and try to keep us down; hitting us every time we try to stand back up, that is satan. God wants us to come to Him for forgiveness, and then keep moving forward in life.

*"He forgives all my sins and heals all my diseases" Psalm 103:3*

Is there something that you have done, or are doing, that you know God is not happy with but you are afraid that if you admit to what you are doing that God will somehow be angrier with you? Are you afraid that if you admit to a sin that you will crush a close friendship? Are you afraid that if you admit to a sin that your spouse will leave you?

_____

_____

_____

_____

_____

_____

Remember this- God already knows everything that you are doing or thinking and He already loves you so much. Admitting to sin is not going to make Him love you any less, but it will give you an opening to begin to get healing for that sin. Admitting to sin is not going to push real friends away.

If someone truly loves you for who you are, they will probably be hurt, but in the long run, they will stick by your side and help you become your best self.

I do believe that it hurts God when we are sinning. When we stop what we are doing, and give it to The One who can help us, He is joyful.

God wants to help us, but we are often too stubborn to let Him in.

Once you begin to let God in and help you with your sin, you will become even closer to Him. You can begin rebuilding relationships with others who have been hurt along the way.

*"But when we confess our sins to Him, He is faithful and just to forgive us our sins and to cleanse us from all wickedness" 1 John 1:9*

I challenge you now, take a moment and pray about any sins you have in your life that you have been pushing back into a far corner of your heart because you are afraid of what will happen if you admit to them.

Ask God to take full control of every area and every corner of your heart.

Give everything to Him and I KNOW He will honor you for that.

After you have prayed about this, take a moment and figure out an action plan to help you change so you don't just slip right back into the same pattern. Be proactive. Be intentional. God has such an amazing life for us to live, full of blessing, if we only get ourselves out of the way and let Him take full control.

Notes:

_____

_____

_____

_____

_____

_____

_____

_____

_____

_____

_____

_____

_____

_____

_____

_____

_____

_____

_____

_____

Father God, today I pray courage and strength over those who are coming to You to ask forgiveness for where they have been. I know You are a kind and understanding Father and that You truly do want the best for Your children.

I pray each person would have strength to face the sin they have been hiding, and that they would have the courage to be open and honest about it, both with You and whomever else their sin has affected.

I pray they would not hold the weight of these sins forever, but give them all to You and they would realize and understand that they are a new creation in You. They have new life and they no longer have to own the sins that they have handed over to You.

Help them to understand that these sins no longer define them because You say we are Your special children.

I pray peace over anyone who has ever been made to feel like they are not worthy of love and forgiveness because I know that You _are_ love.

# THREE

*"Saturday night, my friend and I went to Life.Church. I know that I shouldn't be going there, but I really like it and I get so much more out of it than I do at meeting..."*
                                            *-journal entry December 24th, 2012*

By the middle of May 2013, I had been going to Life.Church consistently for about 5 ½ months and I still had not told any of my family. I felt so much guilt about keeping this from my family, but I knew that it would not go over well when they found out. It was just easier to go to Life.Church on Saturday night, then meeting on Sunday morning. I say it was easier, but it was not easy at all, and I struggled with it for months.

*"We went to Life.Church again tonight! I have been 6 times now and I love it! The praise and worship is so awesome! I love that I can just sing to my heart's content. I love how everyone makes me feel so welcome." -journal entry January 6, 2013*

One Sunday afternoon in February 2013, I had really been struggling with it and didn't have any idea what to do. With no one to talk to about it, I turned on the radio for distraction. The first song that came on was "Promises." One line really jumped out at me "...if you're reaching for an answer and you don't know what to do, just open up the pages, let His word be your strength, and hold onto the promises..."

I was searching for so many answers. Should I even be going to Life.Church? Should I tell someone so if I was just totally off my rocker

21

they could get me back on the straight and narrow? I wasn't even sure why I loved going there so much. I just knew that it felt like home for some weird reason.

*"...I have been making some really big decisions about my life. I have already written about going to Life.Church for the last several months, and I am learning so much. I feel happier than I have ever been.*

*But I also feel like it is time that I should be telling my family about it, but I am scared to death to tell them because I feel like they will probably not have anything to do with me after they know, and I do not know if I am ready to make that sacrifice. I also know that it will not only be my family, but also the entire assembly, all of the assemblies, really.*

*But I have gotten so much more out of Life.Church than I have ever gotten out of meeting. I don't know what to do!!" -journal entry April 21st, 2013*

On April 20th, 2013, I finally told my brother and sister-in-law about going to Life.Church. They were very understanding about it, but they seemed scared for me.

Robert told me that he could not condone me going to a "church", but he could not condemn me for it either as he could see how happy and peaceful I had become.

He could see that I was out from under all of the rules of the assembly and finally able to just build my own personal relationship with the Lord.

He did tell me at that time that going to a "church" was not something that he was comfortable doing, but that was okay with me. This was about me sharing with him where I was at, not me trying to convert him.

I did feel a little better having at least told someone about where I was. I also decided to tell my youngest sister, Meg.

Every time I thought about telling Dad and Mom, I got sick to my stomach.

A few people really pushed me to tell, but others understood how scary that thought was.

On May 5th, 2013, I decided that I was going to be baptized sometime that summer. I also decided to tell all of my immediate family before I was baptized.

My oldest sister, Allison, and her family were in town visiting for a couple weeks over Memorial Day, and I decided that I would tell my family while she was here.

On Memorial Day weekend, I decided that I was going to take a step out of this comfort zone I had created for myself and tell a couple from the assembly who I was very close to.

I had been very close to this couple most of my life and felt they would be ones in whom I could trust and confide.

I thought if I told them first maybe they could be there for support when I told Dad and Mom.
I was wrong.

Every Memorial Day weekend, we have a huge "Christian camp" where all the nearby assemblies get together for 4 days straight. Most of the ones from out of town stay at the local people's houses. I ended up with a family of 3 in my little home for the weekend, making it very difficult to get out to go to Life.Church.
I finally snuck out for a couple hours on Saturday to volunteer at the church gathering items for the Moore tornado relief project.
After I had done as much as I could to help with the relief effort, I went up to the LifeKids area and started talking to my friend, Jessica. I told her that I was going to start telling some of my family that I had been attending Life.Church. I told her I was really scared about it because I had no idea what the reaction was going to be, I was 99.9% sure that it wasn't going to be good.
Jessica told me that she wanted to pray over me before I went back to camp. She got some other leaders together, huddled around me. They put their hands on me and prayed that I would have the strength and courage to tell my family, and that my family would have open hearts.
I have never experienced anything like that before in my life. It was amazing. I grew up in a Christian environment, but I never had anyone care enough to pray over me when I needed extra strength. It was an amazing moment that I will never forget.

I went back to camp very encouraged and confident that I could share with this couple what was on my heart.
"Why is this such a big deal?" Well, let me tell you.
In this Christian group where I grew up, it was either their way or the highway. You follow the rules, excuse me, the "guidelines", that have been set before you, or you are one that has "walked away." When you are one who has "walked away," no one will have anything to do with you... even your own family. I was having a really hard time deciding if I was ready to burn that bridge.
Because of the relationship I had with this couple, I felt I should be able to tell them about attending Life.Church, and how freeing it was to serve God without all the rules and regulations. I thought it would be safe to tell them how I had learned to pray to God like He was sitting right beside me, listening to every word. I was praying, like never before, that they would understand.
It was... an epic fail.
Okay, maybe not epic, but it was not very pretty. It was like they thought

that Life.Church was a drug to which I was addicted. They tried to show me they would support me and "help me through it".

They told me that they would "hold my hand while I figured this out."

During the conversation the husband made a very upsetting comment. He told me, "God was not in Life.Church." It was not for him to make that call. God says that He is where "two or three are gathered," not where "two or three are gathered *in the meeting hall*".

They totally missed the point that this was a choice that I had made; past tense. I was just letting them know because I valued our relationship... a relationship that ended that day. I have not heard from them since.

Their reaction broke my heart. These two people have told me they love me, but love doesn't walk away at the first disagreement.

The pain of the past flooded me when I realized that I had been rejected, again.

It hurts to realize how quickly a relationship can diminish just because we go to different churches. Our God is bigger than that! God is bigger than just being stuck within those four walls. We are serving the same God, and it truly makes me sad that we cannot have a relationship because I choose to serve Him at a different location than you.

My God is bigger than that!

*"...Every time I try to write, I start crying again..."*    -journal entry June 2, 2013

It was a warm, Sunday afternoon on June 2nd, 2013. I decided it was time to I tell my family about attending at Life.Church, even if it was the last thing I did (and I seriously wondered if it would be the last).

It was the final weekend Allison would be in town. It was time to get it all out in the open... for better or worse.

That morning in meeting, I was sick to my stomach for the entire hour and a half message. I talked myself out of it 38 times but always came back to, "I can do this!"

After meeting, I asked Dad if I could come over for lunch, which was weird enough because I have never felt comfortable inviting myself over to Dad and Mom's. Robert invited his family over too. He knew I was planning to talk to Dad and Mom, and he wanted to be there to support me.

I ran into town to get drinks and chips. On the drive back to Dad and Mom's house, I was praying over and over.

It was time to be open about this, but I was still so afraid. I kept praying that if God did not want to me to open this door, to please let me know. If I was going to burn this bridge for no reason, please stop me, but God gave me peace. I knew I was doing the right thing.

Dad grilled hamburgers and hotdogs for lunch. Time was standing still. I was so nervous.

Finally, everyone was out on the back porch eating and everyone, but me, was talking.

A little side note here – When our family was all together, there were 10 adults and 8 kids, and it usually happens that everyone was talking at the same time.

I usually remain quiet because it seemed I never had anything to say that anyone wanted to hear. I would usually just help take care of the kids and keep my mouth shut. I knew this time it was going to get very awkward just trying to get everyone's attention so I could talk.

Meg and I were sitting on the porch swing. I only made it through two bites of my hamburger and felt sick again.

I leaned over and asked Meg, "Is this what the last supper felt like?" Laughing didn't help my nerves so I decided that I better just get it over with.

"Ummm, I need the floor a minute!"

Well, that got their attention. Then Mom said, "Uh oh! Who is your boyfriend?" I decided that I would go ahead and break the ice with "Yeah, I'm pregnant."

Apparently, that would have been better news for them to hear, because everyone chuckled a little bit. Then I said, "I have been attending Life.Church for the last 6 months or so and I love it".

DEAD SILENCE – You could have heard a pin drop.

In my head, I was trying to decide if I should start running, or puke… right there. I couldn't breathe. It was the longest 10 seconds of my life.

Everyone started reacting at once.

Dad, he just walked away, literally, went inside the house without saying a word.

Mom said, "I understand." I don't know what she meant by that because those were the last words she would speak to me for weeks.

My brother-in-law told me how wrong it was to go to a "man-made organization" and that I was not right with God. He told me that I could not run away from my problems like this.

Allison told me that if she could face the struggles she was facing, then I could face mine without having to go off to another church.

They were all missing the fact that this had nothing to do with the assembly, but everything to do with me building my relationship with God. My own personal relationship. No one else's relationship.

After a few minutes, people started heading back inside. I went in and helped clean up the kitchen.

I was praying that Dad walking away had just been an initial reaction and that if I stayed there for a little while he would come around and talk to me. But it didn't happen. For months.

As I have mentioned before, Dad and I have never had a relationship, so I do not understand why it hurt so badly for him to totally reject me like that, but it did break my heart.

Even though Dad and I rarely ever even say "hi", there was something about knowing that he wasn't talking to me that hurt me so deeply. I feel like it is a hurt that I will never fully forget.

I left Dad and Mom's house after lunch and drove into town, crying all the way. I didn't know what else to do. I needed someone to be there for me, but I had no one.

I went to the coffee shop and tried to write in my journal like I did with everything that upset me, but every time I tried to write about what happened, I started to cry again.

I texted Justin, a friend of mine and told him briefly what had happened. He replied, "Well, Anna, hopefully he will come around… you are a good Christian woman with great morals and ethics, and you are as sweet as a peach. Your dad can either realize that he raised a great, independent Godly woman and be over it or he can realize that he raised a great independent Godly woman, who, because of his selfishness and pride, he doesn't get to have a relationship with. Remember this, no matter what, you are an individual, and you are responsible for your happiness. Stormie and I are behind you 110%!" It was just what I needed to hear. I needed to know there was someone in my corner.

The transition from being "in" the assembly to being "out" of the assembly has been very hard, but at the same time, very freeing.

As I mentioned earlier, it was a very strong "our way or the highway" mentality so when I started being at the meeting hall less and less, I expected people to call and say, "Hey, are you doing okay? I haven't seen you." But no, no one called until it was very obvious that I was "walking away." Then one or two brave ones called.

The couple that I had first told about Life.Church, because I felt close to them, have never once called to check on me.

One man called a month or two later, made a lot of small talk, and then said, "So, Richard said that you are going to Life.Church?", and I knew it was on. He wanted to know if the music was "loud" and "had a beat to it" and I couldn't help but smile thinking about JT dancing around the stage, singing his heart out.

That day, the guy who called cautioned me against believing everything that I heard in church. When I told him I was hearing a lot of truth, he said that there was always a little bit of truth in the bigger lies.

He also told me that I would not have the close relationships in a "church" that I had in the assembly. I am so thankful to know that I have proved him wrong on that point. As I was going through this time in my life I was seeing just how many relationships were conditional, and based on the fact that I did was I was supposed to do in the assembly. They were based on me going to meeting consistently, helping in the kitchen, or helping a mom with her children since I did not have any of my own. Everything in the assembly was based on works. Since I have been out of the assembly, I have built so many relationships that are really true friends. I know there are a number of people that I could call, day or night, and they would come help me if I needed them.

I know this about my friends because they have already shown me that they are here for me. I have relationships now that I didn't ever think were possible.

On Sunday, July 7th, 2013, I decided to go back to the assembly for meeting. I don't really know why, but I just felt like it was the right thing to do. When I had told Dad and Mom about attending Life.Church, I had told them that I was not "leaving the assembly" but I wanted to see what else was out there. I felt maybe visiting them at meeting would help them to accept my decision.

I was still not 100% sure that I was doing the right thing by walking away from the assembly, but after that morning, I was sure I had done the right thing.

Dad and Mom barely acknowledged me the whole time I was there. It hurt very deeply.

My Grandma, whom I was really close to for many years, including the time I lived with her when Grandpa died, would not even ask me how I was doing.

The most painful moment that day was when I was talking to my sister. Richard walked up and started talking to my sister, ignoring me. As he walked away, he just looked at me, not saying a word, shaking his head. The rejection hurt so deeply, but it helped me decide right then, if that is how I was going to be treated, I was done.

I have not been back to the meeting hall since, and I don't ever plan to go back. Too many painful memories reside there, and there is no reason to go back to that pain.

Although it hurts that I am not welcome there, I have found so much peace and joy in the freedom of not being there.

*"God is our refuge and Strength, always ready to help in times of trouble"* Psalm 46:1

Has there ever been a time when you had a relationship that forced you to burn a bridge and move on?

While I was going through this difficult time with my family, my pastor gave a message series on Elijah. I can vividly remember him talking about how Elijah was told to leave everything he knew and go to where God was leading him. He didn't leave the barn and plow behind intact, ready for him if God's plan didn't work out. Elijah had so much faith that, not only did he leave everything behind, he slaughtered his oxen, tore apart his plow, and used the wood to cook the oxen meat to share with the village.

This message was confirmation that I had done the right thing. I had burned my bridge, turned my back on an unhealthy past, and followed God.

It is always very painful leaving relationships or things behind, but God wants us to follow Him with our whole heart. Sometimes we can't do that until we come to terms with unhealthy influences in our lives.

I am thankful that a few relationships from my past have been rekindled. We are even closer as we both grow closer to God.

I am confident that if you seek God with your whole heart, He will show you if there are relationships, or things in your life that have come between you and Him.

Have the faith of Elijah!

Notes:

_____

_____

_____

_____

_____

_____

_____

_____

_____

_____

_____

_____

_____

_____

_____

_____

_____

_____

Father God, today I pray guidance and courage over those who are seeking You as they cleanse their heart of people or things that have gotten between You and them.

I pray healing over their hearts where people have rejected them for following You. Help them to understand how much You love them, even if there is not one earthly person that loves them. Help them to feel Your comfort.

I pray they would have faith on their journey and to live life to its fullest, knowing that true freedom comes only from You.

I pray we will all have forgiveness in our hearts for those who have hurt us in the past, and I pray they will open their hearts and see the hurt they are causing.

_"You will know the truth, and the truth will set you free" John 8:32_

# FOUR

## HONOR THY FATHER AND THY MOTHER

Let me tell you a little more about myself, how I grew up, and all that, blah, blah, blah.

My great, great-grandfather was… I'm joking. I am not really going to go back that far.

My mom is from Iowa. My dad is from Oklahoma. They married in August of 1979, and had 6 kids.

Robert was the first born and the only son (I know, poor guy, right?!). Two years later came Allison. Three years after her, Katie was born but only lived for eleven days because of a heart defect. A year later, I was born. 15 months later, came Charlotte, and seven years after Charlotte came Meg.

I was born at home in the little town of Rocklin, just outside Sacramento, California.

We moved to Oklahoma when I was three years old so I have no memories of living in California.

I grew up north of the little tiny town of Luther in a singlewide mobile home. Yes, all seven of us lived there for approximately ten years.

We were all home schooled, such as it was. The only school I can remember doing before high school was a 3rd and 4th grade math book and probably 3 spelling books. So you get the picture, I didn't have much schooling at all, and I was always very ashamed of my lack of education.

The only other girl my age that I knew well was Richard's daughter Julia. She came from a family of two daughters, both adopted. They were very strictly home schooled; up at 7:30, doing school by 8:00, finished by lunch, do your assigned chores, and play for a couple hours in the afternoon. Family dinner was promptly at 6:00, and the day was always wrapped up in the living room as a family.

Although I was always embarrassed by how little school I did as a child there wasn't much I could do about it. That changed in high school.

When I was 17 years old, I enrolled in a correspondence course through a Pennsylvania high school. They sent me the books, and I took the tests online.

Because I was enrolled at an older age, I would graduate at 21 years old. I was so not going to let that happen. I was already embarrassed enough so I took matters into my own hands.

Because it was a correspondence course, I was able to go at whatever pace I wanted. I completed four years of high school in six and a half months. Yeah, you heard me right. Six and a half months.

As long as I live, I will never forget the day I finished. I had gone to Texas with my cousin after Memorial Day weekend. I was in the bedroom and had submitted the final test. It came back with a passing grade! I went running and screaming through the house.

I was so excited and very proud to be graduating at 18 years old! I would not recommend this schedule to anyone. I don't really feel like I learned anything, but I got my diploma, and at the time, that is what counted.

I was the first one of us kids to actually complete high school. I wondered for a while if it would make Dad and Mom proud of me, but it didn't.

Once I was done with school, I worked for Dad in his dirt construction business for a few years, helping him drive equipment, clear lots, and haul brush.

Not a very feminine job, I know, but I would make the most of it. I enjoyed driving the truck and trailer, between Edmond and Luther, windows down, singing to my heart's content.

Some days I was on the tractor, brush hogging or doing a final grade.

One winter, we completely trimmed out a large house. That was an interesting job, and I really learned a lot.

*"I don't know that I can live in Dad and Mom's house until I am old enough to get married. It's so hard to live with people that don't even want me here. I don't feel loved or accepted at all"* -journal entry June 26, 2003

*"It is so hard to be respectful towards Dad and Mom!"* - journal entry August 24, 2003

*"I am feeling a real peace about the possibility of moving to Richard and Gloria's house*

*but I am afraid to tell Dad about it because he is going to be so mad! The other day, Dad threw the weed eater across the barn because it wouldn't start... what is he going to do when I tell him that I want to move out?"*     *- journal entry September 14, 2003*

When I was 19 years old, my younger sister, Charlotte, got married. Richard told me that, since I was already 19 years old, I would probably never get married so I should probably go ahead and decide what I was going to do with my life. I got my first real job at a bank in Edmond. I started as an evening and weekend teller. Over the next eight years, I moved from teller, to new account rep, to a branch supervisor, and then to the IT department.

So far in this journey of mine, I feel I have grown and bettered myself, but none of it has lessened the rejection from my parents. This has been the hardest part.

There are times when I really feel like I have gotten a handle on it and moved on. But then I hear a song on the radio about a daddy and his daughter. All of the old pain reappears.

Many times it is a struggle between the pain of my parents' rejection and also the pain of all the times that Richard has pushed wedges between my parents and me.

I never recognized it growing up, but I can see now, as an adult, how much power Richard had over me, and even controlled how I viewed other people, especially my parents.

*"...this morning when I was leaving the house for work, I saw that Pat (the horse) was stuck in the cattle guard...Dad and Mom started yelling at each other and Mom started yelling at Dad and told him that if he didn't change the way he was talking to her and that if he gave her "that look" again, she was going to walk inside and he shouldn't bother asking for her help ever again. It really upsets me when they yell at each other. I know that I should be used to it by now, but it really bothers me. And then they didn't speak to each other the rest of the day. I hate how it feels around the house when they do this." -journal entry June 11, 2011*

Dad and Mom have had trouble in their marriage for as long as I can remember. On several occasions, Richard, as the minister, has tried to help them, but sometimes, when Mom would go to Richard about things Dad had done wrong, Richard would ask me what was really going on at home. I always tried to tell him, as truthfully as I could, what was going on, and my perception of the situation.

There were many times when Richard would go back to Mom and tell her what I had said. If it didn't match up with Mom's story, Richard would then come back to me and ask why I was lying to him.

This happened many, many times. It always hurt so badly because I told the truth as I knew it.

I wasn't lying. I just had a different point of view than they did. It really bothered me that Richard always thought that.

In the winter of 2004-2005, Dad bought an old, very beat up boat for a couple hundred dollars. We spent the winter fixing it up and getting it ready for the summer.

We completely gutted the boat, replaced the seats and carpet, rebuilt the transom, and fiber glassed and painted the whole boat.

We made a lot of good memories that winter, working in Grandpa's shop, sanding, painting, singing, sanding, scrubbing, sanding, laughing, and did I mention sanding?

Grandpa would walk out to the shop to check on our progress. Grandma would bring us Dr Pepper and cookies every now and then.

It was just a fun family project.

That summer, we took the boat out several times and created even more good memories. One of the very first times we took the boat out, I was skiing. Suddenly the transom started coming loose. The boat went back into the shop for a couple more weeks, and then we were back at it. We would go skiing, even in the rain, or just take it out for an hour or so in the evening.

Of course there were times we would get out to the lake and shove the boat off the trailer, only to realize that something was wrong with the motor. We would load the boat back up, headed back to the shop.

Times with the boat were some of the few times that our family really got along and had fun. And then Richard stepped in.

He didn't feel the lake was a good environment for us to be spending time as a family because, at the lake we would see worldly people (anyone that did not go to the assembly). They would not be dressed modestly, and he just didn't feel like going to the lake was something that we should be doing as Christians. Dad didn't see anything wrong with it, so one day I asked Richard, "If Dad thinks that it is okay for his family to go skiing at the lake, what am I supposed to do with that?"

Richard told me at that time that even if Dad decided his family was going to the lake, I was still responsible for my actions. I could just stay home, and my conscious would be clear.

I struggled through more than one summer, not knowing what to do, not knowing whom to believe. It was hard because when we were all at the lake, I felt like we actually had some good family time, but then I would feel so guilty for wanting to go.

We all know the verse in Ephesians chapter 6, verse 2, *"Honor your father and mother…"* I never knew what to do with that verse.

I wanted to obey God's commandments and honor Dad and Mom, but I didn't know what that looked like.

It took me several years to learn more about the difference between honor and respect, and to realize that it is possible to still honor my parents, even if I do not respect them.

Since I told my parents about attending Life.Church, and I have seen their reaction to that decision in my life, it has helped me learn how to see the difference between respect and honor.

*"Tonight, I went back to Dad and Mom's for dinner to visit Allison and her family before they go home, and Dad and Mom ignored me all evening. It hurt so badly to be in their house and have them not even talk to me. I feel like it made it awkward for everyone. If this is how it is going to be, I don't think that I will be going back over there until Dad has gotten past this…"*　　　　　-journal entry June 19, 2013

Since that day in June of 2013, I have only heard from, or seen my parents on very rare occasions. Every one of those occasions has been painful and uncomfortable.

Dad and Mom did not talk to me at all for several months after I left the assembly, including when I went back over to their house for dinner to see my sister one more time before she went back to Virginia. The whole time that I was there, they completely ignored me so I didn't stay very long.

I saw Dad and Mom again on July 4th, watching fireworks at the college. Once again, Dad acted as if I was not even standing there. It hurt so badly and I just didn't know what to do with that.

The very next day, on July 5th, 2013, Dad texted me while I was at work and asked if I want to meet him for lunch. I felt so many emotions trying to decide if I should go.

Excitement that he wanted to see me again.

Hurt that he had ignored me for the past months.

Anger that he could decide when he wanted to be nice or not.

Scared that he was going to break my heart again.

And over all, I felt like I *had* to meet him because he is my father and I needed to honor him.

We went to lunch, and it was a very awkward 30 minutes. I had an hour long lunch break but lunch was so awkward that I ended up leaving early. Even as we sat there across from each other at the table, we barely spoke at all because we had nothing to talk about.

The only thing that Dad did talk about was trying to get me to come back to the assembly.

It made me very sad to realize that any semblance of a relationship we had was based on what church I attended. It was probably gone for good.

After lunch with Dad in July, I didn't hear from him for another several months.

In January 2014, I saw Richard and his family at the coffee shop one evening, and without even thinking about it, I walked up to him to say hi. He reached out and gave me a hug and we talked for a few minutes. Later that evening it was as if a switch flipped and I felt anger like I have never felt before. I do not tend to be an angry person, but after I saw them again, I was so angry. I began to realize how he had hurt me and so many other people. Then he had the nerve to give me a hug and act like he was glad to see me, when the last time I saw him, he completely rejected me to my face. I really wasn't sure what to do with this emotion because I have never really struggled with anger before. I decided I should just go to sleep, and it would probably be gone when I woke up the next morning. I was not so lucky, and I struggled with this new emotion for days. Finally, I decided to write a letter to him because writing things out has always helped me deal with any emotion. I decided that I really wouldn't have to mail it, but it would be good to just write it out. So I wrote a letter to Richard, explaining some of the things he made me believe about myself. I shared with him how I have grown in my life and in my walk with God, and all that I had been learning. I finished by telling him that I forgave him for all the things he had said to me, and after feeling responsible for feeling bad about myself for years, I was handing that responsibility back to him, so I could live free and happy, out from under the weight that the assembly had placed on me. I told him that I prayed for him to feel the peace from God that I learned to feel.

Writing the letter did help, but knowing he would never see it just wasn't doing the job. I didn't want to be hateful, but for so many years, Richard has held me under his thumb, and I needed to be heard. I needed him to know I had learned to stand up for myself, and defend myself. I prayed about it for a couple days and decided to send the letter. I prayed all the way to the mail box that if this was not what God wanted, that somehow He could stop the envelope from getting to Richard.

It was such a huge weight off my shoulders to verbalize so many hurts, and also such an opportunity to share with him where I was now. I prayed that God would use the letter for good and not for spite.

In February 2013, I was at church, bagging popcorn for 30-second theology weekend. Dad called to tell me had heard about the letter I sent to Richard. He was very upset by it. He said that the letter was full of lies and that I was being very dishonest.

That was discouraging because I had really been at peace since I had gotten that hurt out of my heart, but I had to remember that I was not fighting against Dad. Satan was using Dad to fight against me.

*"For we are not fighting against flesh and blood enemies, but against evil rulers and authorities of the unseen world, against mighty powers in this dark world, and against evil spirits in the heavenly places."* Ephesians 6:12

I have to believe that Dad is being controlled by Richard. I always try to keep that in the forefront of my mind when I am dealing with the hurtful things Dad does and says.

After that day in February, I didn't hear from Dad for another 3-4 months. Even now, it is very rare that I hear anything.

One time, in spring of 2014 I will never forget. Dad asked me to go to lunch with him, and we got to talking about some of the things he was not okay with me doing; wearing jeans, earrings, makeup, etc. He told me that if I had any questions, he would always be happy to meet with me and talk to me about those things, but he "could not, with a clear conscious, socialize with me, on any level".

Those words hurt me deeply because I knew that I was being shunned.

A week or so later, my older sister was in town visiting from Virginia. She called and asked me to come out to Dad and Mom's for dinner. I told her that I couldn't because Dad didn't want me there. She called me back a couple hours later and said that there must have been a misunderstanding because Dad said that I had misunderstood what he had meant when he said that. I told her exactly what he had said and she said okay.

Dad called me that evening and said that he wanted to come into town and talk to me, so I had Robert meet us at my apartment because I wanted a third person there if Dad was going to start going back on what he had said.

The three of us sat in my living room and talked for about an hour. Dad said that he hadn't literally meant that he didn't want me around (not real sure how else you can take "I will not socialize with you", but whatever). This was also the conversation when Dad told me that I had left behind anything good that I was raised in, I had quit attending meetings at the meeting hall, and I had totally changed by cutting my hair and wearing earrings.

It just helped me to understand a little more about how rule-based the assembly is.

It has taken a long time, and I do not have it all figured out even now, but I have to remember that I can obey God and honor my parents without compromising what I believe.

Honoring them does not mean that I bow to their every wish. Honoring them does not mean that I wear what they want me to wear, say what they want me to say, or go to church where they want me to go to church.

To honor my parents, for me, means staying away from the meeting hall and not causing strife. I do not rub my decisions in their faces, but I also believe that I have the right and privilege to live the life that I believe God would have me to live.

I also believe that respect is earned, not given. It has taken me many years to understand that it is okay, although sad, that I do not respect my parents.

For most of my life, I felt like it was my job, as their child, to respect my parents, but I never had any reason to respect them.

Respect is not something that you get just because you are a parent. You must earn that privilege.

My job as a Christian is to live my life striving to be more Christ-like, and to serve my God with everything that is in me. It is not my job to make others happy by following the rules that they have set.

*"For when I tried to keep the law, it condemned me. So I died to the law-I stopped trying to meet all of its requirements-so that I might live for God. My old self has been crucified with Christ. It is no longer I who live, but Christ lives in me. So I live in this earthly body by trusting in the Son of God, who loved me and gave Himself for me"*
*Galatians 2:19-20*

Many people refer to the Lord as our heavenly Daddy, but I have always struggled with that one. I cannot explain the hurt that I have felt, being let down by two different father-figures in my life. I believe that has contributed greatly to my struggle with understanding the Lord's love for me.

If my own father, my own flesh and blood, doesn't want me, love me, or need me, why would my heavenly Father want me, need me, or love me?

I know that He has many more lovable children out there. After all, I was only created to replace Katie and I couldn't even do that.

But oh, if I could have only known how much God truly loves me and wants me.

If only I would have known that He would have died on the cross for me, even if I was the *only* one.

I cannot even explain how exciting it has been the last couple years realizing how much God loves me.

God loves Anna, just for being Anna.

God *wants* to be a part of my life because I am His special treasure.

And God loves you *just as much*! Even if you have been rejected over and over in the past, there is One who will never, ever reject you and He wants to be your very best friend. He has stuck by your side every moment of the way, even if you didn't realize it.

*"But the Lord stood at my side and gave me strength…"*    *2 Timothy 4:17*

*"The Lord is my strength and my shield. I trust Him with all my heart. He helps me and my heart is filled with joy"*            Psalm 28:7

There are those of you who have been hurt over and over, whether physically, emotionally, or mentally, and you know you can never trust anyone again, but I can promise you this, God will never hurt you. He wants to be your strength when you can't stand on your own. He wants to be your comfort when you have no one to turn to. He wants to be your guide when you don't know which way to turn. He wants to be your shelter when everything is crashing at your feet.

He already loved you even before you were conceived. He loved you and He had a very special plan for your life.

Lean on Him and I promise that He is One who will not fail you.

Notes:

_____

_____

_____

_____

_____

_____

_____

_____

_____

_____

_____

_____

_____

Father God, tonight I pray strength over those who are trying to find the courage to trust You with their hurts. I want them to find the joy that I have found by trusting that You really do love each of us.

I pray peace over anyone who has ever been made to feel like they are not worthy of love. Please remove that thought completely from their mind.

I pray defeat over all of the negative words that have been spoken to so many of God's children and have caused years of hurt and sadness.

I pray victory over each one of God's children who have realized just how much God truly loves each of us.

I pray understanding over all of those who need their eyes opened to God's love. I know that You, God, can touch those who need Your healing.

I pray those who have been hurt by hateful words would have forgiveness in their hearts and that they would remember that we are all capable letting satan use us for evil.

Thank you for helping me see and understand Your love for me, and help me know how to share that truth with others.

# FIVE

## YOU ARE A WORLD CHANGER

*"So much has been going on in my life the last month that I want to write about, and some of it will explain why I am writing in my journal during meeting. I am really only here to try to keep the peace until I can decide for sure what I am going to do… In my heart I feel good about what I am doing (attending Life.Church). I am not leaving the assembly because anyone has offended me or upset me, but I want to leave because when I attend at Life.Church, I feel like I am becoming stronger in my relationship with God. People in the assembly don't hesitate to admit that there are more Christians in the world than just those that meet with us, but they aren't 'right' unless they met with us at the meeting hall. I don't get that. It's not fair, and I don't think that it's how God would have us look at it.*

*I keep thinking about if/when I decide to tell anyone about going to Life.Church, who all it will affect. That is where I hesitate to say anything. I feel like there are going to be so many people disappointed in me and I am too much of a people pleaser. But I know that I cannot keep going to the assembly just to make everyone happy."*

*-journal entry April 21, 2013*

April 22nd, 2013 was a really big fork in the road that started me on this amazing journey.

It was the Open Door event at Life.Church, and I had heard Pastor Chris talk about it before. It sounded really neat, but I just didn't think I needed to go meet all the staff and be pressured into "joining" their church. Finally,

41

one day in April, I was sitting in my car, eating my lunch, looking on the Life.Church Facebook page and I saw that they had added the Open Door event. Before I let myself think about it, I clicked "join"… oh shoot! What have I done? That was such a bad idea! Will it show on my Facebook page that I have "joined" a Life.Church event?! Maybe I should just "un-join" real quick?

Then I decided that no, I should just go. Besides, it was during the week and no one should be trying to make plans with me on a Monday night.

That Monday night came around and as I left work and drove to the church, I was so nervous. I had a hundred thoughts running through my head.

I parked over in the west parking area, not too close to the door. I turned my car off, shaking. So many battling thoughts ran through my head as I sat there.

I had been attending Life.Church for a few months at this point, but I had gotten really good at sneaking in, sitting for an hour, and sneaking back out. Wanting, but too scared, to talk to anyone but my friend I was attending with. Wanting, but too scared, to ask questions of anyone. Wanting, but too scared to let someone care about me. I knew that if I let anyone get to know me they would also see that I was not a good person and then I would lose those relationships, too. I would see people who I felt like would really care about me, but I didn't want to be hurt again, so I just snuck in and out. Because I was afraid to let anyone in, I didn't know anyone in the building on that Monday night.

As I sat there, battling with all the thoughts and feelings and fears, I decided I just couldn't do it. I could not go in there and feel awkward and unnoticed by people who *look* like they cared. I have lived with that all of my life and it would just be easier to continue sneaking in and out, pretending they are all super nice, caring people. It wouldn't hurt so badly.

On top of all of those fears, everyone I saw walking into the church for the event was a couple. Okay, I am usually pretty comfortable with being single, but *really?!* I didn't want to feel awkward and be the only single person in the room all in the same night. It was just too much so I started my car and I was putting it into reverse when I heard a still small voice saying, "*stay.*" To which I promptly replied, "I can't! It will be too weird and I don't want to feel like the oddball here, too."

But at that moment I felt God telling me, "Have faith, be strong, and I will be with you."

So I turned my car off again and I went in, every step feeling more scared than the first. I felt like it took me 15 minutes to walk into that building. When I walked in, I wasn't really sure where to go, but figured out that the door was on the other side of the Toon Town room, so I stopped at the little counter and got a name tag. Then I walked in the door and froze.

There were people milling everywhere and from what I could tell, they all knew each other. I didn't know anyone and all I wanted to do was run and hide, and maybe shed a few tears, because I do that some times.

I recognized Pastor Chris from seeing him on stage several times, but I sure wasn't going to go up and talk to him, he was the *Pastor*, for cryin' out loud.

I have no idea what I looked like standing there, but I felt like a sore thumb and I wished that I had never come. I decided that I would at least grab a bite to eat while I was there, and then if I still felt this awkward, I would go home.

I ended up getting in line behind Wendi, and when I saw her, I felt like I had met her before. We finally realized that I had met her 2 days before at the Host Team orientation. We talked while we were in line. She asked me how long I had been attending at the church and what church I had come from (which at that time was really hard for me to explain, but is always a conversation starter). We sat at a table with 3 other ladies who were attending the event and also 2 other staff members: Anne and Jenn. We all introduced ourselves and then they played a video about how Life.Church was started.

Chris got up after the video and introduced the staff. I remember thinking that they really did sound like a fun group of people.

We were then given 10 minutes to discuss, around our table, how we came to Life.Church, and why we stayed there. At our table, there was a lady who said she was raised in a broken home and, even though they went to church, she didn't know if she was saved. Her mother was there with her. She did not attend Life.Church, but had come to this event because her daughter hadn't wanted to attend alone.

During the course of the evening, Chris asked questions of the whole group. One lady asked about being baptized. This caught my attention because I had been thinking about the whole "baptism" subject.

I had been raised to believe that you do not get baptized. To be baptized was something that they did back in the olden days and now it was just a "showy, churchy" thing. No more questions, you just had to be okay with that. But a few weeks before, I had attended church at the Edmond campus on a Sunday morning, and it happened to be baptism weekend. It was so awesome! I knew it was not an act for salvation, but it was such an amazing, outward symbol of being cleansed from your old ways. It was a really awesome experience to watch, but I knew I could never actually be baptized because it was still a churchy thing, and we don't do churchy things.

So, when this subject came up at Open Door, I was thinking, "Oh man, I am going to get some answers about what this place believes about baptism. If they believe you have to be baptized to be saved, then I am out of here. Pronto."

About that time, the LifeGroup/LifeMissions pastor got up and shared some information about LifeGroups, and what each of us will embrace as a next step, so we discussed that at our table. The lady across the table from me was talking about how to get plugged into a good, solid LifeGroup. It was awesome that Anne was at our table as she is on the LifeGroups team and she was really able to answer a lot of questions. Wendi and I talked about how my next step would be to start serving on the Host Team since I had just gone through the orientation a couple days before.

An awkward silence settled over our table as we sat there and watched everyone else talk. So, at that moment, I decided to go out on a flimsy little limb and blurted out, "Can you tell me more about being baptized?" I shared with them about the overwhelming feeling that I got while watching the baptism at the Edmond campus, and I shared things I had been told all my life about how it is not something that we should be doing. I also made the comment that it would be really weird to get baptized without any of my family there. Of course, that led to the question of why my family wouldn't be there for me. I tried to explain that none of my family even knew I was attending that church, and that I had no intention of telling them any time soon because I knew if I did tell them, I would not be accepted into my family anymore.

I remember Anne saying she was really proud of me for being willing to open up and be honest with them, and for just being myself. That comment went a long way with me. No one had ever said they were proud of me for just being me. I have always been told that I am annoying, or I talk too much, but never, "Good job for just being who you are."

The evening was wrapped up with a couple announcements and a prayer, and as soon as "everyone said… amen", Wendi turned back to me and started asking more questions about my feelings concerning baptism. How did I feel about it? What do I believe about it? What were my fears?

As we sat there and talked, everyone started cleaning up and tearing down tables, and then JT, the worship pastor, came over and sat down on the other side of me, and said, "Hey Anna, what's up?"

My first thought was, "You are the important singer dude on stage, why are you talking to me?" and my second thought was, "Wait, how did you know my name?"

JT started asking me a lot of the same questions Wendi had asked. I think I repeated myself a lot, but I was so overwhelmed at this point. I was finally realizing just how much these people really cared.

JT asked me about my parents not knowing that I was attending Life.Church, so I tried to explain the situation as well as I could. I told him that if I told my parents I was attending that church, I would be cut out of my family and would not be welcome any longer. I was almost in tears just explaining it, and then JT placed his hand on my shoulder and said, in a serious voice, "Anna, I believe that God can do an awesome work through you to help your family." I actually kind of chuckled when he said that because he had no idea how ridiculous that idea was. I am not even important enough to my family to know that they love me, much less that I could ever be a help to them.

I remember thinking, "Why am I scared of losing my family when they don't even really want me around anyway?"

I really felt like JT understood that I was not ready to tell my family yet. That was very encouraging because I was having many doubts about whether to tell my family or if I should just scrap the whole church thing all together. I had also been dealing with some pressure from a few other people to tell my family *now*, but I just wasn't ready.

But after that night, I left the church with more information, more hope, more courage, and more importantly, a huge peace that I was doing the right thing.

I felt that God was saying, "Go My child. You can do this. You can become the real you." I had no idea what that was yet, but I would soon learn there was so much about myself that I didn't even know yet.

*"…I have been dealing with some doubts about if I am doing the right thing or not, but*

*after my conversation with JT and Wendi last week, I have felt a peace that I have never felt before."*     *-journal entry May 1, 2013*

On August 12<sup>th</sup>, 2013, three and a half months after my first Open Door event, I went to my second Open Door, only this time as a completely different person, and playing a completely different role. I was so anxious and excited all day waiting for it to be time to go to the church.
 I couldn't help but smile as I parked in nearly the same spot as before. I walked into the church feeling confident and ready to give someone else that warm welcome I had received only months before. I didn't walk in feeling alone and scared, but instead, I walked in to a room full of people greeting me by name and saying, "Hey, thanks for helping out tonight!" I walked in to a room full of people asking me how my week was going. I walked into a room full of people who love me, care about me, accept me for who I am, and push me to grow deeper and stronger.

*"I cannot even describe the feeling of joy that I feel when I see someone walk in who looks uncomfortable and I have the opportunity to show them Christ's love by just being friendly and welcoming. Only three months ago, I never would have walked up to someone I didn't know and introduce myself and ask how they were doing. Only three months ago, I didn't feel near as comfortable talking to the staff and helping them with the event.*
 *I am so thankful for where God has brought me in such a short time. It hasn't always been very easy, but it has been so amazing to learn so much about myself, and the Lord's love for me."*     *-journal entry August 12, 2013*

Backing up a little to April of 2013, a friend had encouraged me to visit the Edmond campus of Life.Church some time, and the weekend of April 21<sup>st</sup>, I finally stopped by. When I had decided to visit there, I had no idea it was baptism weekend.
 As I have mentioned earlier, I was raised that you do not get baptized because it is something that was for the bible times and only "churches" do it now because they think is a requirement to get to heaven. That was that. That was all of the information we needed, and you don't ask questions.
 But I couldn't deny I felt an emotion when I saw the joy on the faces of those being baptized that April afternoon. I can't even explain the emotion I was feeling, but I knew that I wanted to find out more about baptism. Over the next month or so, I talked to a few different people about it.
 I realized that maybe the assembly had it wrong all these years. Maybe it

was okay to show others, by this act of baptism, that you are a new creation in Christ, and you are dedicating your life to Him.

In early May, I decided I was going to be baptized in August. For me, it was not because I was a new believer, as I had been saved as a child, but it was an act to symbolize all I was leaving behind, all I was washing away. I had become a completely different person because of the choices God had been helping me make to leave the old things behind and pursue this new life He had for me.

Baptism was set for August 4th, 2013. I was so excited and a little nervous. I still hadn't told my family about attending Life.Church at this point and I was really nervous what would happen if they found out about the baptism. I knew it would just make a bad situation worse.

I had purposed in my heart that I would be open and honest with all of my family about attending Life.Church before I was baptized. Regardless of the outcome, I wanted this to be a fresh start and a new beginning.

JT came up to me in the lobby one Sunday, about three weeks before baptism. He had heard I was going to be baptized and wanted to know if I knew who was going to baptize me. I told him I hadn't even thought about that part of it. Then, JT asked if he could be the one to baptize me, and that meant so much to me. He has been such an encouragement through this whole crazy journey ever since I met him.

August 4th finally arrived in a flurry of activity. I was also taking the Chazown workshop that afternoon. Chazown is a workshop through the church that helps people find what their purpose is. About 5 minutes before the end of our session, the speaker said something about having to wrap it up for the day so everyone could get ready for the baptism that evening. On those words, I got the shakes. I was so nervous.

Part of the nervousness was that I started doubting, again, that I was doing the right thing, and what would people in the assembly say if they knew I was about to be baptized.

In part, the nervousness was because I can be a complete klutz. I was about to be in front of hundreds of people, and I was so afraid that I would somehow inhale water or slip and fall or something equally humiliating. At one point, I started imagining what would happen if I slipped on the ladder and hit the side of the inflated pool, somehow flooding the lobby. Finally, I stopped for a moment and prayed, asking God to give me peace and quiet my mind.

*"I love the Lord because He hears my voice and my prayer for mercy. Because He bends down to listen, I will pray as long as I have breath!"*      Psalm 116:1-2

Another part of my nervousness was excitement. Excitement about what I was about to do. Being baptized had become a big deal to me and I was ready to take this step.

As we all gathered in the East Room before baptism, I felt a little awkward because everyone in there had at least one or two of their family with them. I was all alone. Then Jessica came in and sat with me to be my "family". For many people that would be a very small thing, but it was very special to me. Another special moment was when Teena came in and told me Steve had prayed for me in the Host Team huddle and that they would all be there to see me baptized.

Once the worship started in the auditorium, we all filed out by the big pool set up in the lobby. I was completely overwhelmed by those who had gathered around to cheer us on. Although I had no physical family there, many people there meant more to me than my family ever has.

I was very focused as I climbed up the ladder and over the side of the pool, and I didn't even trip once. Once it was my turn to be baptized, I walked up in front of JT and instantly plugged my nose, making everyone laugh because I was way early on that part. It made me relax a little. Chris spoke to us for a moment and then it was time.

I came out of the water with huge smile, and a minor slip, which almost took JT and me both down, but I was so happy. JT gave me a huge hug, and I climbed back out of the pool.

My feet barely touched the floor when a towel was handed to me and someone was hugging me, and then someone else was hugging me, and then another. It was such an amazing feeling. I realized that afternoon I had a new family. The kind of family I used to wonder if I would ever have.

*"For we are God's masterpiece. He has created us anew in Christ Jesus, so we can do the good things He planned for us long ago."*      Ephesians 2:10

Something I have learned along this journey, with much help from the special people in my life, is that I am a world changer. You are a world changer.

At the Open Door event back in April of 2013, the people there helped me start thinking about what I really was in Christ. Those people who helped me start believing in myself, and realize that I can be a world changer.

I sincerely pray that each one of us will realize the potential we have to be world changers, and that we would embrace it.

You are a world changer. You may not work at a church, but you can be a world changer in whatever place you are in.

If you are a stay at home mom, you can be a world changer to your children and husband. You can lead your children and be an example to them, raising them to understand they are special and loved and they, too, can be world changers. You can support your husband and be world changers together.

If you work in the work force, there are so many opportunities to be a light for your co-workers and so many others you encounter in your everyday life. I know we have to be careful in this day and age talking about anything spiritual in the job setting, but if you live your life as you honor God, it will show to everyone around you.

Sometimes any of us can get discouraged, and satan uses those times to make us feel even worse about ourselves or our circumstances, but if we pray to God for strength, He will *always* be there for us.

I would encourage you to take a moment each morning to pray and ask God to be with you through the day and that He would give you the opportunities throughout the day to be a world changer. But I will caution you, if you ask Him for opportunities, He *will* give them to you, so be ready!

*"Search for the Lord and for His strength; continually seek Him."* 1 Chronicles 16:11

*"Now all glory to God, who is able, through His mighty power at work within us, to accomplish infinitely more than we might ask or think."* Ephesians 3:20

Notes:

_____

_____

_____

_____

_____

_____

_____

_____

_____

_____

_____

_____

_____

Father God, today I pray courage over those striving to be world changers for You. Give them strength that they will be bold.

For those made to believe they do not matter, I pray that You will show them how much they truly matter to You. Help them see that You have a plan for them.

I pray anyone too scared to stand up for what they believe, would feel Your strength and be able to stand on faith.

Father, I pray others will realize they are world changers, too, and they would embrace that.

As I have written this chapter, I have been overwhelmed by all You have done for me, and I have to take a moment to thank You, Jesus. Thank You for giving me strength and peace when I came to You.

Thank You for putting these people in my path that they would be able to help me see what You were doing in my life.

Thank You, Father, for loving me as Your own special child.

# SIX

## TRUST

Trust: Firm belief in the integrity, ability, or character of a person or thing; confidence or reliance.

How many times have you heard, "You can trust me."? I have heard this many, many times, but that is not how trust works. Trust is not given, it must be earned.

Trust can be earned, or it can be broken.

Writing in a journal has always been very important to me from a very young age. It is a safe outlet for me to process my feelings, dreams, and fears.
 When I was about 12 years old, I found Mom and my aunt reading my journal. You might say, "Really? You were 12 years old; your mom has full right to read your journal. Besides, you don't have anything very private to write about when you are 12 years old." But I would disagree. She would need to read it if I was a troubled child, and she needed to find out what was going on for the safety of myself or others. She read it just because she wanted to. To this day, she doesn't think she has done anything wrong. She broke the trust I had in her.
 She violated that safe place for me. As I grew older, I was always very careful to keep my journals put away because I felt like a child again,

wondering who would read my journal.

Trust is a very tender thing. When there is trust between people, it can make a relationship blossom and become something great. When that trust is broken, it can ruin a relationship, sometimes forever.

*"Trust in the Lord with all of your heart, and lean not on your own understanding. In all your ways acknowledge Him and He will direct your path" Proverbs 3:5&6 NKJV*

*"In God I trust and am not afraid. What can man do to me?"* *Psalm 56:11 NIV*

There is One in whom we can always trust no matter what is happening in our life.

My family had horses all of my life. When working with a horse that doesn't know you well, you have to build trust.

One winter when I was about 17 years old, one of our stallions bit one of the colts on the neck. We didn't realize the damage until several days later, when Stormy, the unbroken colt, smelled like he was dying. He would just go lie somewhere, and we couldn't get him to eat or do anything.

When Dad called the vet out, he said that it would probably be better to just put Stormy down. Dad asked if there was any chance at all that Stormy could live. When the vet said yes, I begged Dad to give me a chance to try to heal Stormy. Dad said yes, he would give me a little time to try, but if the horse didn't improve, we would have to put him down. The vet cleaned the wound. It was about the size of my hand when completely open and deep enough that I could see his throat. I could put my hand in, under his throat and feel him swallow. The vet gave me instructions how to clean the wound and said that it had to be cleaned twice a day, every single day. He gave me a cream to put on the wound, as well as an antibiotic to put in Stormy's feed each day.

I put Stormy in a smaller arena so I could keep an eye on him. Every single day, twice a day for three months that winter, I went down to the arena, cleaned the wound, and spread the cream on it. Then I would put a rope on Stormy and make him walk around the arena. The first week or so, I literally had to drag him around the arena. We would only make a lap or two, and I would let him stop.

Stormy had no will to live. You could see it in his eyes, but twice a day I would make him walk. I would make him live another day. I talked to him the whole time, telling him I was taking care of his wound and that I was making him walk to give him a chance at life. We soon became friends. As he healed, he would walk a little longer and a little faster. Eventually, he started getting up and walking towards me when I walked through the gate.

When all of this happened, Stormy was not broke, so I took advantage of the situation. Once he started getting stronger, I added little things to our walks. At first, I added a bridle, which he got used to pretty quickly. Next, I added a saddle blanket and soon after, I put a saddle on him. He was strong enough to handle the saddle, but still weak enough that he never put up too much of a fight. He had also learned to trust me, and as long as I talked him through any of the new changes, he handled them pretty well.

Three months after his first visit, the vet returned, and he was amazed at the progress. He had not expected Stormy to make it at all, much less doing as well as he was. The vet told me that day that I had saved Stormy's life. He told me that anyone could have applied medication to the horse and followed all of the directions, and the horse probably wouldn't have made it, but because of the love and care that I had shown to Stormy, his life was saved.

Stormy and I continued being friends after that, and there were so many days I would go down to arena and walk Stormy and tell him all the things were going on in my life.

Once he got stronger, I was able to get on the saddle and ride him. He never bucked me off even once, but no one else could ever ride him.

That horse was awesome. Even after he was healed and back to his normal strength, he would always come up to me. He trusted me because, over a period of time, I showed him that he could trust me.

Then one day, I came home and I found out that Dad had given him away. It was a very sad day for me. I felt like I had lost a friend, and I never got that attached to another horse.

Are there relationships in your life where someone has broken the trust? Were you able to rebuild that trust?

Something I have had to learn is that trust cannot always be rebuilt once it is broken.

As I started to lean on Richard, in place of my dad, I learned to trust him. For many years, I believed that he was a good, solid, healthy person in my life. I trusted him so much that, when things got rough at home, I considered living with their family for a while. I remember one night, Dad and Mom were hollering at each other in their room and I called Richard and said that I was going to walk to their house because I couldn't live at home anymore. I trusted him until I realized that he didn't believe me when I would tell him things, and he constantly asked me why I was lying to him. He didn't trust me, and I didn't trust him anymore. I started realizing he didn't think I was worth anything either.

*"Today, Richard texted me and asked me to go to lunch with him, and it was super awkward because we just sat there trying to act nice to each other. He said that he wanted us to just talk so I can tell him everything that I am thinking and feeling and he won't argue, but just listen, but I don't see the point in it because if he doesn't believe that I am telling the truth, what is the point? I really don't know what to do at this point!"*
*-journal entry April 14, 2010*

For a few years I didn't trust anyone. Who wouldn't give up on me once they knew what a bad person I was?

This even followed me into Life.Church. The first few times I spoke with Pastor Chris, I had a bad gut feeling. I couldn't put my finger on it. I didn't even realize for a while that I was uncomfortable around him. One day, I was in the office at Life.Church, and Chris walked up behind me and placed his hand on my shoulder. I jumped and could not even respond to his, "Hello." I felt so bad because he hadn't done anything to make me feel uncomfortable, but it was just a reaction. Finally, one day Chris asked me why I was afraid of him, and I honestly couldn't answer. I had no idea.

Because I do not like to just have reactions to things, and not know why I am feeling the way I am feeling, I really began to think about this. I realized something that Chris said to me a few weeks before sounded like something Richard would say. Chris had said an entire sentence of encouragement, but my brain had locked in on one comment, and it had triggered something in my head.

The next Sunday, I found Chris and I told him, "I figured out why I have been scared of you!"

He asked why, and I told him that it was because something he had said reminded me of someone in my past who had hurt me over and over.

Chris looked at me and said, "I am not that person, and I will prove it to you." And since that day, he has proven it. He didn't just say, "You can trust me." He had to show me, and I learned, over time, that I could trust him.

*"When I met Chris, and told him that my family doesn't know that I have been attending Life.Church, he put his hand on my shoulder and told me to tell him when I am ready to take that step so he can be there for me. It really meant a lot to me"*
*-journal entry Dec 24, 2012*

More than trusting people, we have to learn how to trust in God. We have to learn how to hand everything to Him and have faith that He will handle it how He sees fit.

*"Let all that I am wait quietly before God, for my hope is in Him. He alone is my rock and my salvation, my fortress where I will not be shaken."* *Psalm 62:5&6*

*"I have such a hard time waiting quietly. It is so hard to trust sometimes. Is He really going to do something great through me? I pray that all the things I have gone through in the last couple years can help me help someone else. I pray that I can do great things through Christ. I don't know how to do that, or how to get started, but that is where my heart is, and I am trusting that God will show me what He wants me to do."*
*-journal entry April 24, 2014*

What are some areas in your life you need to leave with God? Make a list of the things you are worrying about, but you need to leave at His feet. You know, He *wants* to take the burden from us.

*"Give all your worries and cares to God, for He cares about you."* *1 Peter 5:7*

When you make your list of things you are going to give to God, place it somewhere you will see it each day. And when you give these things to God, don't take them back. Leave them with Him.
I know for myself, I have a really bad habit of struggling with a burden of worries for far too long. When I finally submit myself and give the burden over to the Lord, within five minutes, I have claimed the burden back and I am worrying about it again. That is not God's desire for us. He wants to carry that burden for us. Let go, and let God handle it. He is fully capable, I promise you.

Is there a relationship where someone has broken the trust you had in them? Is it a trust that can be rebuilt?
I know trust cannot always be rebuilt, but remember this:

*"The thief's purpose is to steal and kill and destroy. My purpose is to give them a rich*

*and satisfying life."*          *John 10:10*

Satan wants to destroy relationships, and if he can do it through broken trust, he is happy with that. God wants us to have a rich and satisfying life, and I believe that good, solid relationships are a part of that rich and satisfying life.

If you have a relationship where the trust has been broken, pray and ask God to help you know what He would have you do. I truly believe that He can help you know if it is a relationship that you should walk away from, or if it is a relationship you can rebuild.

*"...but with God, all things are possible."*          *Mark 10:27*

Is there a relationship where you have done something to break the trust of the other person? What have you done to correct it? Have you asked them to forgive you? Have you asked God to forgive you?

God wants us to come to Him, and I believe that He forgives us over and over. I am so thankful God is not finished with any of us. He is still working on us, and He knows we are human and will mess up.

*"And I am certain that God, who began the good work within you, will continue His work until it is finally finished on the day when Christ Jesus returns."* *Philippians 1:6*

What is your game plan to change what you did before so that you can begin to build that trust back? What are you going to do differently?

Trust is such a fragile thing, yet it can become so strong.

I would urge you now, take some time and ask God to show you the relationships where you need to work on trust, whether it is in building your trust in someone, or someone building their trust in you.

Spend some time asking God to show you the areas you need to trust God to take care of you.

Are you still looking for a job? Is your marriage struggling and you don't know what is going to happen? Are you a couple that wants to have a child of your own, but you haven't gotten the results you wanted? Are you single and you wonder if God really has a special someone for you? Are you a parent, staying up late, waiting for your child to get home? Are you a child, wondering if your parents even wanted you?

I know there are so many more situations than I can even imagine, but I do know that God knows about every single one of them. He cares about every single person out there who calls out to Him to find peace. He is the One you can place your trust in, and He will never break that trust.

Notes:

_____

_____

_____

_____

_____

_____

_____

_____

_____

_____

_____

_____

_____

_____

_____

_____

Father God, tonight I pray peace over the ones coming to You with a heavy burden. I pray You will remove the burden from their shoulders, and You will carry it for them.

For all of the ones who are too scared to trust, I pray they will see that they can place trust in You, and You will never break that trust.

I pray courage over the ones who have realized they have broken someone's trust, that they would be able to go to the person they hurt, ask forgiveness and that they would be able to rebuild that relationship. Help them to remember You are not finished with us yet.

I know satan wants them to not rebuild the relationships, but I pray Your strength over the ones truly trying to make things right.

I pray healing over the ones who have trusted someone, only to have that trust betrayed and broken. Heal their hearts and help them learn how to trust again. I pray they would remember You forgive us for so much every single day, and they would have forgiving hearts towards those who have broken their trust.

Father, I pray surrender over those worrying about things they cannot do anything about. I pray they would hand that over to You and have peace.

I pray healing over the hearts that have been broken, and the spirits that have been smothered. I pray strength over those who have been made to feel weak.

Father God, help us each to be more like You every day.

# SEVEN

## WE ALL HAVE A SPECIAL CALLING

*"When you realize who you are in Christ, He can use you in ways you never imagined*
*-Markey (August 20, 2013)*

One of my favorite things I have learned over the last couple years since I have been free from the chains of the assembly is that I have a special calling. I have talents, and there are things I am good at.
I know this may sound boastful or prideful to some, but I believe there is a time and place to have a healthy dose of pride in yourself.
As you have probably figured out from the first two chapters of this book, I was not raised to have any confidence or pride in myself.
I never believed that I was good at anything, or would ever be good at anything.
I never knew I was actually good at several things.

I have always loved to serve people, and to make things easier for them. A lot of times this came out in ways of helping people prepare meals on "potluck Sundays" in the assembly. I especially enjoyed helping moms with young kids by either preparing their meal for them, or taking care of their child while they prepared the meal. It has always felt very natural to me to take care of people. There were times after I started to really believe I would never have a family of my own. I thought maybe this is what I was created for, to help others take care of their families.

But I couldn't seem to do that right either. I remember, it was May of 2011, and I was in charge of making coffee and keeping a hot supply on the tables at a friend's rehearsal dinner. It didn't work out so well. The dinner was out in the far corner of someone's yard so we had strung power cords out to the site. When I went to make the coffee, the power was not enough for the commercial coffee makers I was using so the coffee ended up being mostly lukewarm, dark water.

I didn't know any of this was going on with the coffee because I had gone back to the house and boiled water for hot cider, but when I got back over to the rehearsal site, several people were stressing out. Some people thought it was tea because it was so light.

I had no idea what to do. I never made coffee, much less in a commercial sized coffee maker. I eventually figured out what had happened with the coffee and I took the coffee maker and plugged it in at the front porch.

I felt awful and knew that I had failed completely. I had one simple task: make, and keep warm coffee for the visitors, and I couldn't even do that correctly.

*"Anthony helped me carry the coffee pots back up to the front porch and once we plugged them in, they began to percolate right away. But by the time we got the coffee done and back to the rehearsal site, everyone had finished dessert and some were even leaving already. I finally went back up to the house because I was just so discouraged and I was fighting tears. On my way back to the house, I passed George and Sherry and they had been up at the house and had made their own coffee. It just made me feel that much worse. I hate it when I get emotional over stuff like this, but I feel like every time someone is counting on me to do something, I fail.*

*I ended up just staying up at the house and helping another lady clean up the kitchen and wash all the dishes. There were also 4 other ladies standing in the living room talking and I realized that they were talking about the coffee fiasco. And about the same time, someone carried in the coffee pots, because most everyone else had left, so I asked Sherry what I should do with the two, almost completely full, pots of coffee. She told me to dump it out because it wouldn't be good and that it was a waste because everyone was done by the time it was made.*

*I told her that I was sorry for wasting so much coffee and that next time someone asked me to do something like this, I would just tell them no. She replied, "Well, now you know." Then she turned back to her friends in the living room and was snickering about what I had said.*

*Do they not realize how badly their words hurt? I know that I am not able to do stuff like this now, and I will not agree to try anymore, but they don't have to make fun of me, especially while I am standing right there!*

*This evening has reminded me too much of Allison's bridal shower (when I was 15 years old) and Sherry told me that I was not dressed enough like a lady and that I needed to call Mom and ask her to bring me something nicer.*

*Will I ever be good at anything? I feel like the only thing I am really good at is spending time with my horse, Stormy. I can take care of him well, and besides, he doesn't laugh at me when I mess up."*     *-journal entry May 14, 2011*

Another thing I believed I could do well was playing the piano. I learned to play the keyboard by ear and I was able to play several songs out of the hymnal for meetings. I didn't play often because I didn't think that I could play well enough, but I tried to keep getting better and better.

One Friday night, I played for a while, and thought I had done well. I was asked to play again the next Wednesday night for meeting. When I got up to the piano, Jeff told me, in front of the entire congregation, "Just don't play like you are at a funeral this time".

I was so embarrassed! I had played as well as I knew how when they needed someone, and that still wasn't good enough.

After that, I didn't play the piano in front of anyone for many years because I came to believe I wasn't any good at that either. I still don't claim to be very good at playing, but I do think that learning what I did about music has helped me enjoy singing, and I have had a few opportunities to use that.

Over the last year or so, I have had a few opportunities to sing with Justin and Kim at a small church. I love every moment that I get to sing worship to my God, whether it is in the car or on a stage.

For most of my life I did not believe I was good at anything, but I have been learning more and more about my special calling and my talents as I learn to trust God and let Him show me these things.

Becoming involved at church has really helped me understand that I was, in fact, good at different things.

As I mentioned earlier, I have always had a heart to serve others in a practical way, so I started serving on the Host Team and loved it.

I will never forget the very first Sunday I served, but I will let my journal tell the story of that evening.

*"...When I got to the Host Team room about 5:30, there were a lot of people in there, and they all knew each other but me. I was so nervous! I hate not knowing anyone! I recognized Steve, Teena, and their son, Robby, from the orientation, but I didn't really know them at all.*

*I went on in, got checked in, and then I just sat there, feeling so awkward and wondering if I had done the right thing by agreeing to do this.*

*There was another couple there also, that is engaged, and they had run a marathon that morning. They seem like such a sweet couple. I can't remember their names, but I felt like I had met him before. She said that she thought that she had met me before, but we couldn't figure out where. She decided that maybe she just felt that way because we are destined to be friends.*

*Steve had pulled up a video clip on the TV of a campfire, and Teena had brought a little s'more set. We all gathered around and Steve talked for a minute, and then he made a really big deal of introducing me to the whole group! I know that I turned so red. Next, we each shared a "good". Teena's "good" was that she had met me that day. It really made me feel welcome. After the first few minutes, I really didn't feel like I was coming in on their group. I felt very welcome.*

*That night, I stood at the little drink counter and put ice in a bajillion cups. It was so much fun! I loved standing there, and greeting people that I had never met before, with a smile. I love being able to greet the different people and I want to make them feel welcome, like so many have made me to feel there.*

*When I was finished filling cups, I went back to the kitchen and helped another lady wash all of the drink containers. It was such a fun evening! I can't wait to see what God does with this new chapter in my life..."*            -journal entry May 5, 2013

As spring turned into summer, I spent every Sunday night I possibly could serving on the Host Team. The longer I was there, the more people I met, and I really felt like they became my family.

I still hadn't told my family that I was attending another church. It weighed on me every time that I was there, but everyone was such a huge support to me. There were a few Sundays that our family would have something going on, and I wouldn't be able to serve. I was always disappointed to miss a Sunday evening with them.

On May 12th, 2013, I went up to LifeKids to look into serving with them because I have always had a heart for children. There I met Jessica.

She showed me around and talked to me about what it would be to serve in that ministry. In that conversation, it came out that I had not told my parents I attended that church because I knew when I told them, they would probably never speak to me again.

When I told Jessica briefly about my family, she gave me a big hug (which still kind of freaked me out because I was not a very physical person), and told me to be sure that I told her before I told my family about church because she wanted to be praying for me when I told them.

I didn't know how to respond to that. No one had ever wanted to pray for me before. It really touched me.

Eventually, once I left the assembly and had more time on Sundays, I served in LifeKids on Saturday evening and Sunday morning. For quite a while, I was serving at church for all 7 services. It really helped me during the transition period when I was being rejected by all of my family and friends that I knew, to be surrounded by people I was developing relationships with.

I really loved my time serving in LifeKids, and I learned so much more about myself, and about my strengths.

I loved what I did on the weekends. I would get there early and help Jessica set up the rooms, and then we would usually have a minute to chat and catch up before everyone started arriving for the 5:00 service. I never knew what I would be doing during a service. It would be anything from checking in a new family, rocking a baby to sleep, walking laps around the LifeKids area with a buggy full of toddlers, hanging out with some 4-6 year olds, or pouring into leaders. There was more than one time that I would be carrying a baby in a front pack while I also pushed a buggy or checked on rooms. I also wrote a lot of cards to leaders during that time. Sometimes I would write a card, here or there, as I had time. Sometimes they would have enough leaders, and I would go to the office and sit and write cards.

In August of 2013, I went through a workshop at church called "Chazown", and it is about finding what your purpose is.

It was such a great experience, and I learned so much about myself.

The first Sunday afternoon session I was a little distracted because I was getting baptized at the evening service, and I was really nervous.

The second Sunday afternoon session was amazing and everything felt like it came together and made more sense.

At first, when I was trying to get my core values, my spiritual gifts, and my past experiences to all tie together, I was having a hard time seeing how they all fit together.

Then I realized that the way I had grown up feeling very unloved and unwanted is a very common struggle in girls today. If I could help just one girl know how much God loves her and has an amazing plan for her life, I would give it everything I have. Out of that came my Chazown statement:

*"I believe that God has a plan for me and it is to help young women know how much God loves them regardless of their relationship with their parents (or any past relationships)"*

*"…I do not know what God has planned for my life, or where He is leading my journey, but I chose to use every moment of my life to serve His people with whatever He has given me…"*     *- journal entry August 11, 2013*

I believe God places things in our hearts He is calling us to do, and that could look different for everyone. You may think that you have this thing that you enjoy doing and are just kind of good at, but *what if* that little thing is the thing God is calling you to pursue and to build on?

I believe many of you have something in your heart you have always felt you were supposed to do, but have been afraid to try.

I know that I have. Take this book for instance.

Growing up, one of the things on my bucket list has always been to write a book. I have always imagined that I would write a book about my grandparents, and who knows, maybe I still will someday. About two years ago, Jessica encouraged me to write my story. She said it would be very encouraging to some others to hear about how I had the courage to leave everything I had known to follow after God with my whole life. So, I wrote out several stories, explaining some about where I had come from and what all had happened in my life.

In the time I worked on that, it was very helpful. I know I processed and dealt with a lot of the pain from my past. It was a very emotional time for me.

This last fall, I started thinking, again, about trying to write a book. Many have encouraged me to write a book about my story, but I just didn't feel good about that. I didn't want to write a book about my life, from beginning to end. I am still in my 20's so I haven't gone through enough of life to do that yet. But I was torn because there were a few times where I had the opportunity to share my story with others, and they always told me how encouraging it was.

I brain stormed other ways to share my story in an encouraging and inspiring way, but I never could figure out how. But I just didn't feel like writing a book about myself was the answer.

In October of 2015, the message at church was about having God confidence instead of self-confidence. Something that really stuck out to me was when the Pastor talked about being afraid to do what we are called to do because we are too afraid of failing. As soon as he started talking about that, my book came to mind. I was frustrated because I felt like God was telling me to write this book, but I didn't know how. I didn't think I had enough words to make an actual book. And yes, a big part of it was that I was afraid to fail. I knew that if I did start writing a book I could not tell anyone about it because I would not want them to know if it didn't work out and I had to scrap the whole idea. Then only God would know that I had failed.

One day, shortly after that confidence message, I was spending some time in prayer, and I told God I really did want to follow His leading, but I honestly did not know how to write this book. Then I realized I didn't need to sit down and write a book about Anna's life timeline, but my desire was to write a book to encourage and inspire others and to give them hope. I had been looking at it wrong the whole time. I started to get excited because I knew that, with God's help, I could write encouragement, and I would just use my story as a way to give someone hope.

I was still a little overwhelmed by how to start, so I started looking at blogs and comments online from writers and one person had said to write down 10 questions, then use those as your chapter titles and just use that chapter to answer the question. When I read that, I got so excited and I could barely wait to start. I knew that I could do this.

A couple days later I had a three day weekend and I went to the lake with Robert and Crystal's family and another family that we are close to. It ended up being a rainy weekend, so Saturday afternoon, I grabbed a notebook and a pencil and I just started writing. I couldn't stop. I was amazed by all that God was placing on my heart.

Before I started writing, I prayed over my book. Handing the entire project to God, and asking Him to lead, and He has proven so faithful. That first weekend, I wrote the first 3100 words in two days. I have been so overwhelmed by what God has done with this book. There have been times when I feel like I am out of words and that I cannot go on, and then God puts something more on my heart to share with all of you. I have had moments when I have felt that I am way out of my league, and I have no business writing a book, but I have to! God has called me to do this.

What is your special calling? What has God placed in your heart to do? Have you taken a moment to ask God what He wants you to do and then stand quietly and let Him speak to you?
Is there something you know that you are being called to do and you are afraid of failing? Ask God to help you with that fear and I know He will be faithful to you. He wants you to have a blessed and fulfilled life.

Notes:

_____

_____

_____

_____

_____

_____

_____

_____

_____

_____

_____

_____

_____

_____

_____

_____

_____

Father God, I pray clarity over anyone who is searching out what You are calling them to do. I pray they would have the courage to pursue that calling with everything in them. Help them to trust fully in You and not in their own abilities.

Thank You for all You have already done with this book, and thank You for giving me the courage to pursue writing.

Anna Stamper

# EIGHT

## YOU HURT BECAUSE YOU LOVE

*"Church was incredible today! It was the first time that I have cried during one of Pastor Craig's messages. The message this week was week 3 of the "Bless This Home" series, and Pastor Craig was talking about the difference between a peacemaker and a peacekeeper. A peacemaker works through conflict and a peacekeeper avoids conflict and acts as if nothing is wrong. I know that I am pretty much a peacekeeper, but I want to be more of a peacemaker.*

*The part of the message where I really broke down was when Pastor Craig was talking about how much family matters. He was talking about forgiveness and why would we push someone away only to hang on to the grudge. Because family is everything, and family is worth fighting for!*

*It didn't make me cry because there is someone that I wish would forgive me, but it broke my heart because my family doesn't think that a relationship with me is worth fighting for. I just wish that my family could understand that God is so much bigger than our differences, and He wants us to be there for each other anyway!*

*I really wish that I had someone that I could talk to about all of this. Sometimes I feel like there are so many feelings and thoughts floating around in my head and I can't make sense of it all."*  -journal entry May 12, 2013

It has been two and a half years since I told my family about attending
Life.Church. During that time, I have had very little contact with my Dad
and Mom. So many times I have questioned whether I am doing enough to
make things right with them or if it is really worth it to go to a different
church.

In July of 2014, my older sister and her family were here from Virginia.
One evening Dad and Mom invited all of us kids over for dessert. I debated
whether or not I should go. I didn't want to because every time I had been
around Dad or Mom I always got hurt, and I didn't like how everyone
pretended like everything was okay every time my sister was in town. I
ended up going, but only to support Meg, who still lived at home. It was
such an awkward and uncomfortable evening. Dad and Mom barely spoke
to me.

The next time I saw Dad and Mom was in November of 2014. Shopping
with my niece, we ran into Dad and Mom when we stopped to have pizza
for lunch. It was very difficult to know how to act normal. How do you act
casually around your parents when you only see them every 4-5 months
even though you live only 20 minutes apart?

I saw Dad and Mom again in December of 2014 at Meg and Trevor's
wedding.

I started really feeling like I needed to make more of an effort to reach out
to my parents. I wanted more than anything to show them that I had not
"gone off the deep end." I was still myself, just a much happier version. I
wanted to show them that God's love was bigger than our difference of
opinions about what church was the right church. I did not want to try to
make them go to the church that I was attending, I just wanted them to see
how happy I had become and to accept me as part of the family.

So, in an effort to show them this love, I invited myself out to Dad and
Mom's house for dinner on night in April of 2015. My sister and her family
were here from Virginia so I thought it would be easier than being alone
with Dad and Mom.

They agreed to let me come for dinner, and I prayed continually as I drove
there. I prayed, asking God to give me courage and strength. I prayed He
would be with me if my heart was broken once again. I prayed He would
open Dad and Mom's eyes to see we could be together as a family,
something they were sacrificing because of pride. I prayed for courage to
stand up for my beliefs, and strength to stop Dad from pushing me around.

I prayed for comfort, and to be reminded that He was in my corner. I was very nervous going to their house. I hadn't been there in some time, and every time I had gotten my heart broken.

When I got to the house, I realized my younger sister, still a part of the assembly, was also there with her husband and children.

I wore jeans. Of course, my sisters and mom were in long skirts. I considered wearing a skirt, but I did not want to bow to their ways. I wanted them to be okay with me for being me; the me that I am with confidence from God, not the me that I was told to be.

That proved to be a very hard evening. Dad barely spoke to me all evening. Even my mom and sisters had a hard time finding things to talk to me about. I hadn't seen my younger sister's two young children in some time. The youngest didn't even know who I was. My heart, completely broken, I cried all the way home. I felt like I had to go there and make an effort, but afterwards, I felt it had been a complete waste of time and effort. My family still had no need of me.

I did not spend time with Dad and Mom again until July 2015 when Meg came home from Montana for a visit. Meg had spent the day with Mom, but that evening Meg was going home with me. It was suggested that we meet Dad and Mom in town for dinner. I didn't want to, knowing how uncomfortable it would be, but if they were inviting, then I would do my part and be there. Dinner went well, and we laughed a lot, but through the entire evening, Dad could hardly talk directly to me. It was as if he didn't know how to talk to me. It really bothered me because I wish he could see that I am still Anna. I am still his daughter. But when we are together, he behaves as though we have never met.

That evening, Dad prayed before we ate dinner. He thanked God for the opportunity to have Meg there with us, and then he prayed "and thank You for the chance to spend some time with Aaa.....", and then a very long awkward pause that lasted long enough for me to look up at him and realize he had forgotten my name. It wasn't like he had to run through the list of names of kids because he had gotten me mixed up with one of the other kids, but he had really forgotten my name. He soon settled with, "Well, thank You for the chance to have the girls here with us." It showed that he doesn't often think of me or talk about me. It hurt.

Several times I have seen Dad or Mom in town. It is always painful, and I haven't ever been able to understand exactly why.

Why does it make me want to cry when I see Dad or Mom at an intersection? It isn't like we talked to each other and they were hateful. Just seeing them across the way almost always brings tears to my eyes.

Just last week I was driving to the house of my brother, Robert, not even paying attention to the time, and I ended up driving by the meeting hall right at 10:25am, only minutes before meeting was to start. Driving by just as Mom was turning in, there were several seconds when our eyes met. Then she just drove on. A little farther down the road, I passed my uncle, aunt, and my grandma. It brought tears to my eyes. A little farther, I passed another uncle and aunt and their family.

I don't want to go back to that way of living. I am happier now than I have ever been, and I know I have people in my life who truly love me unconditionally. I wouldn't trade that for the world. So then, why do I hurt so badly when I see them? These people who use to be part of my life?

One day, I finally asked my brother why seeing Dad and Mom makes me want to cry, even when they didn't say anything to me. He really gave me something to think about.

Robert helped me understand that I hurt because I love them.

I have often wondered if I really love my parents. Yes, I love them because Jesus commanded us to love one another, but do I really love them as my parents?

But now I know I do love them. That is why it hurts so badly when they reject me and my beliefs.

The assembly, as a whole, is very rule based, and not love based at all. When they see me, they see I have chosen not to follow their rules, and therefore they are done with me. They do not see that I am following God as I feel He has called me to do. They do not love and support me as I follow God's leading, because I am not following their rules.

I still love my Dad and Mom, and Grandma, and many others still in the assembly, and that is why it hurts so badly when I see them. It is a reminder of their rejection. They are rejecting me and the love God has placed in me. They are rejecting God and the love we are commanded to show to others. They feel they are in a position to decide who is worthy of that love and who isn't.

It hurts so badly that my parents do not want me in their life. I really struggle with it. I wish they could see God's love is bigger than our difference of opinions. God doesn't command us to love only those we get along with, or those we like being around, or those who we agree with. God commands us to love our neighbor.

*"… Love your neighbor as yourself.' No other commandment is greater than this."*
                                                              *Mark 12:31*

I cannot make Dad and Mom want me in their lives. I cannot force them to love me. But what I can do is show God's love to them when I have the chance, and I can show God's love to everyone else I come in contact with. I pray often that God would let others see Him through me. I want my everyday life to reflect the love God has placed in me. I want my words to reflect His love. I want Him to direct my words each day that they would be gentle and encouraging.

*"Do not use foul or abusive language. Let everything you say be good and helpful, so that your words will be an encouragement to those who hear them."*   *Ephesians 4:29*

*"Let everything that has breathes sing praises to the Lord!"*   *Psalm 150:6*

*"A gentle answer deflects anger, but harsh words make tempers flare."*   *Proverbs 15:1*

I have also had to learn that as badly as I want Dad and Mom to be part of my life that may never happen during our life time. I will pray for it daily, as long as I have breath, but it still may never happen. I have to understand that God will supply my every need. God knows how badly I want them in my life, but He has given us our own will, and if they choose not to be in my life, I have to accept that.
In the last few years I have gotten a much better understanding on how much God really wants the very best for us. He will supply our every need if we will only look to Him for our comfort.

*"Show me Your ways, Lord, teach me Your paths. Guide me in You truth and teach me, for You are God my Savior, and my hope is in You all day long."*   *Psalm 25:4&5*

*"The Lord is my strength and my shield; my heart trusts in Him, and He helps me. My heart leaps for joy, and with my song I praise Him"*   *Psalm 28:7*

*"And this same God who takes care of me will supply all your needs from His glorious riches, which have been given to us in Christ Jesus."*   *Philippians 4:19*

God has more than supplied my needs. When I feel as if I have no one to call family, I am reminded that I do have family who loves me, both blood family and "family" who has chosen me. People in my life call every holiday to make sure I am not alone and that I have somewhere to go.

We did not celebrate Christmas in the assembly, so I celebrated the holiday for the first time in 2013. I had more invites than I could accept, and it has been about the same every holiday since.

As much as I wish my parents were involved in my life, I have learned it is okay, and sometimes for the best, to love from a distance. It still hurts when I see Dad or Mom, or think about something that is going on in my life I wish I could call and tell them about, but it has come to a point that, for the protection of my heart, I have to love them from afar. I do love my parents. I am sure of that now, but loving someone doesn't always mean you have to be with them. I pray that one day they will realize we all serve the same God. Even though we may do it a little differently. I pray they will accept me into their family again. I will welcome them with open arms but for now, I have to protect my heart and move on with my life.

*"I don't even know how to explain what I am feeling. I just want to tell everyone, but I am not even sure how I would tell people because it doesn't make sense when I try to explain it out loud, but I am so happy. Sometimes I feel so happy that I want to cry for no reason.*

*I am happy because I feel like the Lord loves me more than I will ever fully understand.*
*I am happy because through God, I have value, even though no human on earth needs me.*
*I am happy because I now have real friends who love me and want me as part of their lives.*
*I am happy because I go to a church where I am free to worship my God how I want.*
*I am happy because I have been given an opportunity to be a light to others.*
*I am happy because I am a child of God!*
*I just wish my family could see me this happy and understand that I have not gone off the "deep end." I wish they could see that I am truly happy, and that they could also have experience this happiness if they could get out from under all of the rules and laws of the assembly. It is so freeing to be happy because God loves you and that is all that really matters. I pray that one day they will be able to experience this happiness also."* - *journal entry July 18, 2013*

Are there relationships that you have severed because you don't agree with the way that they are serving God? Are there relationships that others have severed because of the way that you are serving God?

Whatever your situation is, I want to remind you of a few things.

We serve the same God, even if we do it in different buildings, or in different ways.

Remember that satan is doing whatever he can to separate families, and he knows that how we serve God can be a very sensitive subject to some. He uses that. Let's not let him win.

Remember that we are commanded to love our neighbor as Christ loved us. Those are some pretty big shoes to fill, and I don't believe it is our place to decide who deserves our love, and who doesn't.

Even if you have had people reject you and break your heart over and over, God will still supply your needs. Sometimes those needs are different than we think they should be. There has been more than one occasion when I told God I needed such and such, and He supplied me with something other than I had asked for. I realized He knew, better than I did, what I really needed.

One more thing, don't take for granted the relationships you have around you. If you struggle because you do not have much, or any, physical family, or maybe they do not live near you, take a look around at the family God has given you anyway. Take a moment and sit down and write a list of people in your life who you can trust and rely on. I promise it will overwhelm you when you see all God is doing for you right now.

If you do not have many good, encouraging friends, maybe examine your life and see where you could change it a little, put yourself in a better position to build encouraging relationships. That may look different for everyone. If you are not going to church, visit a few churches and see if you can find one where you feel comfortable, and begin building relationships there. Get involved in some of the ministries that the church offers, and you will be surprised how many new people you will meet and get to know. Find a small group where you can get involved in other's lives and let others invest in your life. It will change your life once you really surrender and let others see inside your heart.

Notes:

_____

_____

_____

_____

_____

_____

_____

_____

_____

_____

_____

_____

_____

_____

_____

_____

_____

_____

_____

Father God, tonight I pray healing over anyone who has been rejected by their family. Help them to find healing in You. Help them know that Your love is bigger than the differences we humans create in our lives and relationships.

I pray strength over those who are learning to move on in spite of relationships they are leaving behind. I know it is painful, but You can give them strength to do what they need to do.

I pray thatYou would guide those trying to get involved in a small group and trying to let people into their lives. I pray You would place the right people in their paths like I know that You have done in my life.

I pray for Dad and Mom tonight that their hearts would be softened and their eyes would be opened. I pray they will see Your love through me.

Thank You for always supplying my every need, and for placing so many amazing people in my life.

Anna Stamper

# NINE

## FEAR

Fear:

*noun:* an unpleasant emotion caused by the belief that someone or something is dangerous, likely to cause pain.

*verb:* to be afraid

*"For God has not given us a spirit of fear and timidity, but of power, love, and self-discipline"*   2 Timothy 1:7

*"Don't let your hearts be troubled. Trust in God, and trust also in Me."*   John 14:1

Do you ever have those nights where you have lain awake in your bed and you feel as if the whole world is crashing down around you? You feel as if everything is going wrong and you do not know how it will work out?
I have. In fact, if we are being real honest here, tonight was one of those nights.
One of my hopes for this book is that the readers will not feel as if I am "preaching" to them, but rather that we are sitting in my living room just having a normal conversation between friends. So, with that hope in mind, I am going to be open and vulnerable with you.
Just tonight, I lay down in my bed, fully intending to go right to sleep and get a good night's rest as I have a meeting first thing in the morning, but my mind would not rest. There have been several nights like this since I have

started writing this book. Most nights I am sleepless because I have a message on my heart I want to share, so I get up and write a chapter.

Tonight was different. Tonight my heart was heavy with fear. I was carrying fear of things I could not control. I was carrying fear of things I have given to God over and over, but once again, chose to take back on myself.

I was carrying a fear of bills looming. I was carrying a fear of being alone for the rest of my life. I was carrying a fear that I wouldn't be able to finish this book and I would completely fail. I was carrying a fear of Meg being so far away as she is nearing her due date.

God tells us in Matthew 11:28:

*"Then Jesus said, 'Come to Me, all of you who are weary and carry heavy burdens, and I will give you rest'."*

God wants to carry our burden and fears for us, but so often we insist on taking them back over and over again. God cares about every one of the fears I was carrying, so much more than I ever could. When I stop and think about it, it really seems silly because I can't do anything about most of these fears. There is no other option but to let God handle them.

Take a moment here and write down a list of things you are afraid of. Be honest with yourself and search your heart. What are you not willing to let God handle?

_____

_____

_____

_____

_____

_____

_____

After you have written down your fears, think about the truth that God *wants* to carry them for you. He asks us to give Him our burdens and fears. Tonight, once I realized that I was not going to sleep because I was stressing out about earthly problems I could not solve, especially in the middle of the night, I got up. I came into the living room and just began talking to God about the fears I was letting control me. Instantly the fears and pressure began to lift.

I know, without a doubt, that God wants the very best thing for every one of His children. I asked God to give me wisdom as I face financial decisions. I thanked God for giving Meg a husband who loves and protects her. I prayed that she would be safe and have a healthy delivery when it is time.

I know I cannot control if I am single for the rest of my life, but I do know that God has a plan that is best for my life. If that does not include a husband, I have to be okay with that and trust God. Sometimes I am guilty of only trusting God with the parts of my life that I am comfortable with. This makes me think of the verse in Psalm 37:4,

*"Take delight in the Lord, and He will give you the desires of your heart."*

As I focus the desires of my heart around serving the Lord with my whole heart, soul, and might, He has in turn made serving Him the desire of my heart. It is a cycle; the more I serve Him, and commit my everything to Him, He gives me the desire of my heart, which is serving Him. I know I am always my happiest when I am serving God and His people.

Last but not least, He knows my fear of not being able to finish this book. This is such a silly fear. I have no goal other to encourage and inspire His people through sharing some of my experiences. There are no deadlines, quotas, or expectations. Honestly, it boils down to the fact that I am a perfectionist, and I want to be in control. I gave this fear back to God, also, tonight. This is not my book. This is His book, and He will do with it as He wills.

I believe that, at times, we can let pride get in the way. We think so highly of ourselves. We believe we can solve any problem or fix anything that is not right.

We give God so little credit for already having our lives in control. He holds our whole world in His hands, so why can He not take these small burdens from us? He knew the situations we would face, even before we were born.

He cares about every single little thing that is going on in our lives. He *wants* us to bring everything to Him. Even the little things.

During those times when you are afraid, and your mind is running wild, just take a moment and ask God to be with you. You will be amazed at the result. I know this because I have experienced it many times. When we pray to God for peace over our unsettled world, He will listen to you. He will calm your fears.

*"Don't worry about anything; instead, pray about everything. Tell God what you need, and thank Him for all he has done."*     Philippians 4:6

Some fears are bigger and can take us down. Leaving us completely paralyzed. That moment a mother can't find her child. An emergency responder's wife gets a phone call. You see on the news there has been another mass shooting, a devastating tornado, a massive wildfire. You hear of a marriage vow that has been broken. A pregnancy scare, or for some, the fear that you will never be able to have a child of your own.
There are so many fears that stop us in our tracks. Fears that make us wonder, "Will we ever come out of this?"
For me, I faced that type of fear the winter I turned 13 years old. We were at my aunt and uncles farm in Luther. There was a lot of snow on the ground for this part of the state, so a bunch of us had gone over there to go sledding. Better known as "red neck sledding"; we were pulling a car hood behind the 4-wheeler. We were all having so much fun, completely carefree.
My dad's phone rang, so he stepped away to answer it. When he hung up, he pulled Mom and my aunt and uncle to the side. I remember seeing their worried faces and wondering what was wrong. Without saying what was happening, Dad told us girls that we were to go home that night and he would talk to us later, but he and Mom needed to leave.
I found out later that evening from someone else that my cousin, Shelly, had been diagnosed with leukemia. Shelly was 11 at the time and she was so full of life. She was a very out-going person and everyone loved her. I remember feeling a very big fear. I didn't know what cancer was, but I knew it had to be very bad by the reactions of everyone around me.
Shelly lived with her family in Arkansas, but they had taken her to St Francis Hospital in Tulsa, Oklahoma for treatment. The night Dad and Mom got the phone call, they drove to Tulsa right away. We girls stayed home that night, then drove up to Tulsa with friends the next day.
During the time Shelly was in and out of the hospital, we made many trips up to Tulsa and back. My younger sister, Charlotte, was closer in age to Shelly, so they spent a lot of time together. Shelly's older sisters were closer

to my older sister's age, so I didn't really have anyone to spend those long days with. Shelly had a baby sister at that time, so I spent a lot of time walking the baby around the hospital, trying to give my aunt a break. I was pretty young so I don't remember a lot about her treatment and what all she went through. I do know that she had a really rough time as she fought the cancer. I remember occasional wheelchair races, pulling pranks on the nurses, and many hours of air hockey in the waiting room.

About a year after Shelly had begun the battle with cancer, she was doing really well. Then she cut her toe while working in the garden. Because her immune system was so low, the cut on her toe got infected and she ended up back in the hospital. We all went back up to the hospital to be with the family, but it was looking very grim. Because of the infection, they had to amputate one of Shelly's big toes. More and more problems kept arising. After some time, Shelly was not responsive, and the machines were keeping her alive. My aunt and uncle had a very hard decision to make, but they decided to let her go. They knew she would never be well again.

By this time, so many people we knew from the assembly came to the hospital to be with the family. The day they decided to unplug Shelly, we all went into her ICU room. As Shelly took her last breaths, we all sang to her. I don't know if she could hear us in those last moments, but I like to think that she could. I like to think that she was not afraid because she knew her family was there with her.

I will never forget that day as long as I live. I was too young to know everything that was going on, and no one told me anything. As I looked at Shelly, lying there, taking her last breaths, she looked so different. I could barely recognize her. I knew that my cousin was too young to be dying, but yet she was. At that age, I didn't understand what cancer was. I only remember for years afterwards, if I got a bruise, I wondered if I was going to die. Shelly bruised very easily, and she died. I was so afraid for so long.

The night Shelly went to Heaven, I remember the drive back home from Tulsa. I cried a lot of the way home. During our time in and out of Tulsa, I had seen a completely different side of Dad and Mom, especially Dad. He had been so caring and involved in all of the events at the hospital. He took care of my uncle and aunt, doing anything he could to make their life easier. I hadn't ever seen him support someone like that. There were times I was very excited because I thought maybe this event had changed him somehow. But it didn't. I knew he was very upset and sad when Shelly died, but nothing changed between him and us kids. I can remember for years after Shelly died that I wished that I would get cancer so Dad would love me like he obviously loved my uncle and aunt, and Shelly.

Fear can really affect our lives. As a child, I had a fear that I had cancer because I didn't know what cancer was. There are so many things we can be afraid of when we don't have all of the information. We have tests run but are waiting for the results. We know someone is in harm's way, and we are waiting to hear that they are okay.

It is in these moments when we have to lean on God. He can handle anything we bring His way and He *wants* to carry the burden for us. Having faith isn't just something we say, but we have to live it out at the same time. It is in these moments of complete fear that we have to put our faith into action.

*"Give all your worries and cares to God, for He cares about you."*     *1 Peter 5:7*

*"Today at meeting, Uncle Kenneth told me that Julia was struggling with something and if she left the assembly, it would be my fault. It hurt so badly. I feel so pointless. I have tried so hard to help and be an encouragement to Julia, but yet I am just told all that I have done wrong. It also hurt really bad that Uncle Kenneth judged me and made me feel so badly without even getting the whole story."*     *- journal entry December 9, 2012*

Another type of fear is fear that others place on us.

In December of 2012, Uncle Kenneth told me that if Julia left the assembly, it was my fault.

I knew that Julia was really questioning the beliefs of the assembly, and she was not sure if she should be there. I was terrified that she was going to leave, and I would carry that guilt for the rest of my life. That was not a fear that should have been placed on me. I am not responsible for the decisions Julia makes.

There have been so many fears Richard has placed on me. Fear of no one wanting me. Fear of never having a happy life if I left the assembly. Fear of living under his judgement.

I know there are many abusive relationships where people are living in fear every day. I cannot relate to that situation, and I am thankful to God for that, but I do know that God is with each one of us in whatever fear we are facing. He can, and will, comfort us when we are afraid. He is there to protect us.

84

*"So we can say with confidence, 'The Lord is my helper; so I will have no fear...'"*
*Hebrews 13:6*

*"Let all that I am wait quietly before God, for my hope is in Him. He alone is my rock and my salvation, my fortress where I will not be shaken." Psalm 62:5&6*

*"My grace is all you need. My power works best in weakness." 2 Corinthians 12:9*

Earlier in the chapter I asked you to write down some of your fears. Looking at your list, are there any fears you wrote down that God is not able to handle?

I am not a parent, but as an aunt, I want the very best for my nieces and nephews. If my 4 year old nephew was trying to carry a very large rock that was too heavy for him, I would run to help. I would *want* to help. I know that he could not handle it, and I would not want him to hurt himself. Imagine how much *more* God wants to carry our burdens and fears for us.

I know I can be embarrassed by fears I let stay in my mind. Sometimes I feel embarrassed to tell God what I am struggling with, but that is silly. God knows everything about me already. He already knows what I am thinking. He already knows what is in my heart and mind.

*"O Lord, You have examined my heart and know everything about me. You know when I sit down or stand up.*
*You know my thoughts even when I am far away.*
*You see me when I travel and when I rest at home.*
*You know everything I do.*
*You know what I am going to say even before I say it, Lord.*
*You go before me and follow me.*
*You place your hand of blessing on my head.*
*Such knowledge is too wonderful for me, too great for me to understand!" Psalm 139:1-6*

How are you going to give your fears to God? I am a fan of action over intention. Don't just say you are going to give your fears to God, because I know, if you are anything like me, you have really good intentions, but you will continue to hang on to your fears, not ever giving them to God.

I will tell you about a little habit I started to help me be more intentional about handing over my fears. I write down each of my fears on a piece of paper. I fold each piece of paper up and place it in a wooden box. I then place the wooden box in my closet, out of sight. I am sure that it sounds

crazy, but I feel like it helps to physically "put my fears away."
Of course, there are times when I still lay in bed and stew over my fears, allowing myself to get worked up again. But every time I do this, I am getting better at stopping whatever I am doing and praying. I take a moment and ask God to forgive me for taking my fears back from Him, and I ask Him to take them from me. I ask Him to give me peace once again. Every single time we are committed to live for Him and we ask for peace, He will give it. God has proven this to me over and over. I have faced countless nights, after leaving the assembly, when I would lay awake at night, wondering if I had done the right thing. Had I burned a bridge I would later regret losing? But through all of the sleepless nights, God has taught me to trust in Him more and more.

Notes:

_____

_____

_____

_____

_____

_____

_____

_____

_____

_____

_____

_____

_____

_____

_____

_____

_____



Father God, I pray peace over those who are living in fear tonight. I know that You are aware of the situations and people who need Your peace.

I pray comfort over those who are scared and hurting. Wrap Your arms around them. Help them to feel Your strength and protection.

Father, I ask You to help all of us to leave our burdens with You. I know You want to carry them for us, and You know what is weighing us down. Help us to let go and rely on Your strength and not our own.

I pray we would all have strength to cast down the fears that keep us from doing what You have called us to do.

*"Teach me Your ways, O Lord, that I may live according to Your truth! Grant me purity of heart, so that I may honor You."* Psalm 86:11

*"Dear brothers and sister, when troubles of any kind come your way, consider it an opportunity for great joy. For you know that when your faith is tested, your endurance has a chance to grow."* James 1:2&3

Anna Stamper

# TEN

## WILL I EVER HAVE A REAL RELATIONSHIP?

When I left the assembly in the summer of 2013, I was told I would never find real friends anywhere else.

I was raised to believe the only real relationships I would ever have in my life were the ones I had with people in the assembly. When I stopped to think about the relationships I had in the assembly, I felt like I didn't really have a lot to lose.

I didn't have a relationship with any of my family, and I didn't really have any true friends. My relationships were not based on a friendship, but on the consistency of my attendance at meeting and the commitment I showed to the assembly.

I was always too much of a country girl to fit in with anyone else my age at the camps we had about four times a year. There was only one other girl my age in the Oklahoma area, and we never got along. I was never as good of a Christian as she was and she reminded me of that often, telling me I would always be insecure because of my family.

I used to see other girls who had grown up in "good, Christian" families with structure and never doubting their parents wanted them, and I was so jealous. They were always the ones who got married at a young age and had the perfect, good, Christian husband. About a year later, they would have cute little kids, and they were the perfect little families. They were never discouraged or upset. They would never randomly start crying when everyone would play a father-daughter game of volleyball, or have a formal father-daughter dinner. I wanted to be those girls so badly.

So, when I left the assembly, I knew I was giving up a chance to ever have a special relationship like that because I knew that once I left, I would never have real friends.

Oh, but if only I had known what I know now!

I wish the person who told me that lie could spend a week with me now. I have so many real friends in my life now that I cannot spend time with each of them every week.

I have so many special people in my life who really care about me. I care about them and would drop everything if they needed me.

I have learned what a relationship really means. A relationship is not about being a "cool kid" or not. A relationship is not about if you can play volleyball or softball good enough. A relationship is not about if you are at meeting every Sunday, Wednesday, and Friday. A relationship is not about who you are related to.

A relationship is two people who care about, and love each other, and are willing to put themselves out there for the other. Even if it means that you get nothing in return.

A relationship cannot be about doing something for someone else, expecting something back in return. A true relationship is unconditional.

*"...I am so thankful God has brought me to this place, and has placed these people in my life. I can't even imagine where I would be, well, yeah I can. I would still be in the assembly, sad, lonely, and frustrated. Trying to follow all the rules and trying to make everyone happy. But now, I have friends who love me for who I am, regardless that I am an emotional dork who says stupid things sometimes, and over thinks everything.*

*I have friends who I can totally depend on. If I needed a room, I could call and go on over. If I needed a hug, they would be waiting with open arms. If I needed a good cry, they would be there to mop up the mess.*

*I have friends like I have never had before. I have friends who are like family."*

*-journal entry October 20, 2013*

I was 19 when my younger sister, Charlotte, got married. I was struggling with her getting married before me because there was so much value placed on being married at a young age in the assembly.

I should also note here that we were only allowed to date within the assembly. That could really be a problem when the very few guys who were actually in assembly were not interested. As you could tell by my story back in chapter 2, the girls were not allowed to pursue the guys under any circumstance, so you pretty much just had to wait and see if anyone decided they liked you.

I didn't stand a chance at all as the guys always went for the girls who were good at sports or had the good Christian families.

There were a couple different guys I was interested in as I grew up, but I never could do anything about it. They always ended up choosing a girl who was better "wife material" than I was.

So, when my sister got married before me, it was very hard for me. Someone had chosen her. I talked to Richard about this hurt I was facing, and he told me I would probably never be married if I hadn't been chosen at this point. Hearing those words, I felt completely hopeless.

I understand now that he had no right to make that judgement, and no girl should ever be told that. But at the time, it broke my heart. I knew he had to be right, but it just left me feeling so pointless. I was still fighting the battle in my mind about why God even let me be born.

I couldn't fill the hole in Dad and Mom's life when I was born to replace Katie. Then if I wasn't to get married, what was there for me to do?

I believed those words from Richard for 6 years. There were times when my sisters had babies, and I would sit and rock them and start silently crying because I knew I would never have a child of my own. I have a heart to care for others, and I wanted to be a mom so badly, but I knew it would never happen. Every time one of my sisters would have another baby, I was always so very happy for them, but there was a tiny part of me that was always sad, too, because I knew I would never have that chance. I have five nephews and three, about to be four, nieces, so I have been through this over and over. We get the phone call saying that someone was going into labor and I would want to cry every time, but would swallow it back. A few hours later we would get the call that the baby had safely arrived and we would all go visit and take turns passing the baby around. I would swallow back the tears. When I got home, I would let the tears fall.

Some of you may think I am weak for crying over this, but it was a very real pain in my heart.

When you believe something, with every fiber of your being, for 6 years, it is hard not to fall back into that lie. There are still times when I fall back into that lie. I let satan get in my head and convince me that I will be alone forever, instead of trusting God. Trusting He has control in that area in my life as much as He has had in the rest of it.

Even to this day, if I start feeling down on myself, or think I am ugly, or even just get overtired, satan knows where I am weak. He brings up that same lie that I will never be good enough for anyone to love me or want me.

*"… Meg called me the other night and told me that Trevor had been messaging her on Facebook and then they started texting, and then they talked on the phone for four hours the other night. He knew that he would be coming back to Oklahoma for a week or so and he wants to see her while he is here. Since she told me this, I have really been struggling. I had a hard time when Charlotte got married, and when Richard told me that I would never get married, but I feel like this is even harder because Meg is eight year younger than I am. She is cute, she's fun, and she's outgoing. I just feel like everything that Richard has ever told me about myself is actually true.*

*I know that life is not about falling in love, but I feel like this is bigger than that.*

*I keep thinking of all of the times Richard has told me that no one will ever want me, and that I will never be good enough. It overflows into my work life and my efforts at church. I feel like I am not a good boss, and that none of the tellers like me. I don't feel like I am making any kind of difference at church either.*

*I know these are lies coming from satan, but they have been wreaking havoc in my heart."*      *-journal entry December 19, 2013*

I really thought I had worked through this struggle and put it behind me. Then my youngest sister, Meg, started dating her now husband in December of 2013. All of those feelings came up faster than you could imagine. Even as happy as I was for them, as they continued dating, I didn't really know what to do about the pain. I still associated it with Richard and the assembly. So it was a whole different ballgame to be still experiencing it even after I had gotten away from that environment, worked through and processed so much of that hurt.

All of a sudden, I felt like that rejected little girl again, and I didn't like it. After several days, maybe even weeks, of praying and seeking God, begging Him to help me understand, I started seeing the truth.

It was the same old lie that Richard had told me all those years ago, and I was letting it back into my life.

One afternoon after spending some time in prayer and really seeking God's truth about me, I decided to make a list of all the lies I was letting myself believe. Then I made a list of the truths God said about me.

I want to share that list with you because I promised myself when I started this book that I would be open and honest about everything, even though it leaves me feeling vulnerable.

I should warn you I get a little passionate as I go down the list.

| Lie: | Truth: |
|---|---|
| I am ugly | I am beautiful. God made me just how He wanted me, even the things I do not like about myself. |

| Lie: | Truth: |
|---|---|
| No one will ever want me | God wants me! God loves it when I acknowledge Him. God would have died on the cross even if I was the only person on earth. |

| Lie: | Truth: |
|---|---|
| I will never be married | That may be true, but that is for God to decide, not Richard McLoser. I AM complete in Christ, all on my own. A husband would be an extra blessing, but not a must have to follow God. |

| Lie: | Truth: |
|---|---|
| I will never have real friends | Ummmm, back that truck up! I can name at least 20 people, right here and now that I can be totally open and be myself with. Okay, so that's close to no one... Seriously?!! |

| Lie: | Truth: |
|---|---|
| I have no real talents, strengths, or gifts | -Writing    -sensing needs<br>-encouraging    -organizing<br>-babysitting    -cooking<br>-sewing    -singing<br>I am responsible, caring, loyal, levelheaded (usually), compassionate, organized, creative, focused, |

observant, intuitive, driven, sensitive, and generous…just sayin'.

| Lie: | Truth: |
| --- | --- |
| I am not making any difference at church | I have greeted people with a warm smile. I make Jessica's job easier by being a second her, and helping things run smoothly. I made a very special quilt for Chris and his wife for Christmas.<br>I can pray for leaders. I can welcome families. I can support leaders. I can brighten someone's day by offering a smile. |

I know these things may seem trivial to you, but they were big lies that I struggled with for a long time. They kept sneaking up on me and trying to take me down again.

*"Patient endurance is what you need now, so that you will continue to do God's will. Then you will receive all that He has promised."* Hebrews 10:36

As many of you know, I am a writer. I know that probably sounds like I am stating the obvious as I am writing this book, but it is more than that. *I am a writer.* When something happens in my life, good or bad, I want to write about it before I would pick up the phone to call a girlfriend.

When I finally got the job that I had wanted, and had been waiting on for months, I wanted to write about it before I wanted to tell someone.

When I broke up with my boyfriend, I wanted to write about it first.

Writing is how I process hurt, joy, and happiness, and I write in my journal all the time. At times, during the last couple months, it has been quite the battle between wanting to journal, and also wanting to continue working on this book.

Because of my love of writing, I love to make lists when I am discouraged about something. There is just something about seeing things on paper that helps me accept them. I believe it helps me to clear my mind of the negative thoughts so I will have more room to fill my mind with God's truths.

Another list that I made one day was a list describing things I am. Sometimes it just helps me to see it on paper, and while writing the list, it really makes me think about the truth of who I am.

I am what God says I am, not what me, or any other human, says that I am.


We all have relationships in our life, whether they are healthy or unhealthy. Sometimes relationships are only for a season in our life.

I want to take a moment to write about some of the good relationships I had when I was younger.

My grandparents on my dad's side lived next door to us, which in our country life meant that they were a quarter of a mile away, but still our closest neighbors. Since I was homeschooled, I had a lot of time on my hands and for several years, I would walk up there every single day to see Grandpa and Grandma. I was especially close to my Grandma and I spent so much time with her.

We spent many hours baking together, whether it was cookies, peanut brittle, butter horn rolls, or many other things we made together, that is where I learned a lot of what I know about baking. Even when I moved out on my own, I would still call her from time to time with a baking question.

There were a few times that we would paint together also. Grandma had taken oil painting classes, and she always enjoyed painting little signs or birdhouses. Grandpa would make little wooden boxes or figurines in the shop, and then Grandma and I would paint them. I still have several of these items packed away.

Sometimes I would go up to Grandma's house and clean her whole house while she sat and worked on a crossword puzzle.

Most days involved a cookie and Dr. Pepper break where we would play Chinese checkers with a wooden checker board and wooden pegs that were painted all different colors. Grandma eventually gave me that checker board, and I feel like I almost go back in time when I play that game.

There were several times I remember confiding in Grandma about things that were upsetting me, usually involving a fight with Dad or a fight between Dad and Mom. She was always a safe person for me to talk to.

I was pretty close to Grandpa, too, but it was different. Grandpa was a little more gruff, so it was more like I didn't realize how close I was to him until he was gone.

I remember when I would go spend the day with Grandma, and we would take cookies and Dr. Pepper out to the shop and have a little break with Grandpa and see what he was working on. He also had a bin full of really old clothes that he was keeping to use as rags, but they had been in there since like 1970, and us girls would play dress up in them.

In September of 2010, Grandpa passed away while we were at a Christian camp over Labor Day weekend. It was a very hard time for me.

A week or so before this, we had gone up to visit Grandpa and Grandma. At that time, Grandpa didn't know who I was. It was really sad. We went up to say goodbye to them before we left for Labor Day weekend because we didn't expect Grandpa to be here much longer. At that time, I didn't even go in and see him again because it was too hard the last time when he didn't even know who I was.

Grandpa passed away on Saturday morning, and we were at the camp in west Texas until Monday afternoon. I remember begging Dad to take us home, but he said there was nothing that we could do at home, and that it would be better to be with our Christian family for the weekend.

It was so hard for me to be around hundreds of people while dealing with this loss. I didn't know this had a name at the time, but I have an introverted personality so I need space and alone time to process things.

Everyone I talked to, most of whom knew Grandpa, kept saying things like "He's in a better place now" or "At least he is not in pain anymore." I knew these things were true, and I was very thankful he was not in pain and that his memory was back. I liked to think about him dancing down the street, fully able to walk again, with his two granddaughters who had gone to heaven before him. But even looking at these things, I missed him, and I needed to grieve. No one gave me a chance to grieve, and I ended up doing that much later on my own time.

That weekend at the camp, I can remember singing Grandpa's favorite song in meeting and completely falling apart. I ended up going back to the dorm, Meg joined me, and we just sat there on the bunks and cried.

I also wanted to go home to be there for Grandma, but I didn't get to go home until Monday. Then I was back to work on Tuesday.

The funeral was on Wednesday, and it was the first funeral I had ever been to. It was awful. I felt like I cried the entire day. Allison and I sang a song at his funeral. It was so hard to make it all the way through without completely losing it, but we made it.

When it came time for the viewing, us kids did not want to walk past the open casket, so Dad let us just walk out the back instead. Some of the family was upset by that, but I am thankful my dad understood that we did not want to remember Grandpa that way.

After Grandpa passed away, I lived with Grandma for 3 months while she adjusted to life without Grandpa. There were so many nights we sat in the living room and read the bible together before bed. It was such a special time. I was also there for her when it was time to go through Grandpa's things and move them to storage. Grandma let me take all of Grandpa's old button up shirts. I made a quilt that I gave to her on her next birthday.

I tell you the stories about Grandpa and Grandma because they were the two relationships I remember as good things from my past. I loved spending time with them.

I am thankful Grandpa passed before I left the assembly because I believe that it would have broken his heart. He would not have understood. Grandma hasn't understood at all, and she hasn't really had anything to do with me since the day she found out that I was attending another church. It hurts me so badly that the special relationship I have always treasured is gone.

*"...My grace is all you need. My power works best in weakness..."*
*2 Corinthians 12:9*

There have been several relationships I have had in my life. Even though they were good for the season, there became a time I needed to move on. Some of those relationships were even after I left the assembly. I met people, and we were a part of each other's lives for a season.

What relationships are in your life? Let's focus on the healthy relationships first. I want to encourage you to invest in them with all of your strength. Give them everything you have. When you are spending time with those people, be present.

Regardless if you are spending time with your spouse, your parents, your children, or your best friend, put yourself in the moment. Put down your phone, or laptop, or whatever is distracting you. If your child comes into the room and wants to talk to you, don't just say ok, but turn off the TV, turn to them and really hear them. *Show* your child they matter to you.

Your response to your relationship can literally change someone's life.

We also have relationships we need to let go of if they are not healthy. If you bring these relationships before God, He will help you know what you should do.

I believe there are some people God places in our lives for a season.

Notes:

_____

_____

_____

_____

_____

_____

_____

_____

_____

_____

_____

_____

_____

_____

_____

_____

_____

Father God, tonight I pray understanding over anyone trying to figure out the relationships in their lives. I pray that You would help them see if they should be moving on or fighting for a relationship.

I pray the parents out there would embrace the children they have been given by You, and they would treasure every moment with them. They would take every chance to show their children how special they are to You.

I pray the couples out there would treasure every moment together and would fight for their relationship together.

I pray that You would empower all of us who are single that we would always remember how much You love us, and that we would remember that is what really matters.

Father, I ask that You would help every one of us that we would be strong enough to face the lies that satan makes us believe about ourselves. Give us strength and courage to tell satan to get out of our way.

God, help us to rest in Your power when we are weak. Help us to remember that You *want* to be our strength

# ELEVEN

## MY REAL FAMILY

I started a list of names of the people I wanted to mention on the "Acknowledgments" page of this book, and I realized I could not just mention these people. So, the Acknowledges page became a chapter.

This list of names I have written down is a list of my *real* family. The relationships I have with these people mean more to me than the relationships I have with my biological family.

These people have helped me become the person that I am today, and they have had a huge part in molding my story.

I am using this chapter to honor those who mean the world to me.

**Robert and Crystal** - I have been close to Robert most of my life and I have always treasured our relationship. When I was young and we lived in our trailer house, there were several times that I would have bad dreams. I would sneak into Robert's room and sleep on the floor. Most nights, he didn't even know that I was there, but I felt safe. In February of 1999, I was almost 12 years old. Robert moved to Virginia, and I had a really hard time when he left. While he was out there, I would write to him and call him as often as I could. I would often look to him when I was upset with something that was going on at home. In March of 2002, I was 15, Richard and another minister from the assembly in Virginia told Robert and I that we could not continue talking about things I was going through because they wanted me to go to the ministers with my problems. I continued writing to Robert, but I was always careful not to mention anything that I was going through. This was so hard for me because I had looked to Robert for answers so many times. I knew he loved me, and he could also relate to how hard it was to live with Dad and Mom.

*"I don't understand at all. I know that the men know what is best for Robert and I, and I hope that I can understand it someday. I don't know why they would take away the only person that I know actually loves me. I wish that I could just go live in Virginia with him. I don't know how to keep writing and talking on the phone with Robert without telling him the truth about what is going on around here. When Robert called me to talk to me about this, we were both crying on the phone. Richard tells me that I need to talk to Dad about my problems, not Robert, but how can I do that when Dad doesn't ever want to talk to me? I guess I will just have to keep writing about everything so I don't bust." -journal entry March 13, 2002*

In April of 2002, Robert married the sweetest woman on earth. I had known Crystal's family for a while so I was very excited she was becoming my sister-in-law.

Robert and Crystal moved back to Oklahoma in December of 2003, and I loved having them back here. A couple years after they moved to Oklahoma, Robert bought some land and we built their first house here. And yes, I mean "we". I would spend any spare time over there working with Robert.

Since they have lived here, they have built 3 houses, and I was very involved in the first couple houses. I would go over and help him, sometime for days at a time. Some of my favorite memories are of us roofing in the middle of the night. One time, we finished shingling a roof in the rain very early on a Sunday morning and hurried inside to get ready to go to meeting on time.

We had so many adventures while working on their different houses. We made so many memories that I wouldn't trade for the world.

*"Today was opening day of deer season for rifle. Robert and I sat together in a two person tree stand that was set up in the far southeast corner of Dad's land. I normally just sit under the tree, but I decided I would give the tree stand a try. It was kind of scary trying to climb into a deer stand 20' off the ground, wearing jeans and a long denim skirt, plus carrying a rifle and a pack.*

*I got up at 5:00am, and we were in the stand by 5:30. We couldn't shoot until 6:30am, and we never saw anything except a couple dogs this morning. At one point, I was resting my head, and all of a sudden Robert said, "Here they come," and thinking that it was a deer, I pulled my rifle (Grandpa's old M1 .30 caliber carbine) up, but I realized Robert was talking about some ducks we had been watching. We laughed about that for a few minutes.*

*We finally went back to the house about 9:30am because we were freezing. We went into town and worked for a few hours. Then we headed back out to the field.*

*Not long after we got back up in the stand, I saw some ducks fly off the pond. Then Robert said, "There it is." I assumed that he was talking about the ducks again, so I just chuckled. Then he repeated himself, and I finally saw that he was talking about a nice little buck. I was able to pull up and get a shot off. He walked about 10 yards and then hit the ground! As soon as I realized that I had hit him, I got the shakes! I started to get up, and Robert said that since it was still so light out that we would stay there a few more minutes and see if we saw anything else. Seriously, not 5 minutes later, another nice little buck walked up, and Robert was able to shoot it!*

*Dad has always had a rule, 'You only shoot once. You should never have to shoot more than once to put dinner on the table'. So, when he heard multiple shots, he texted and asked what all the shooting was about. We replied that we were headed back to the house and we would explain then.*

*It was such a good feeling to get back to the house both hauling a deer! I loved that I got to do that with Robert. While we were sitting in the stand this morning, when we weren't really seeing anything, we had so much fun talking and catching up. Sometimes it seems like we get so busy, but it was really great to get to just hang out and talk like we used to when I helped him on the houses a lot." -journal entry November 18, 2006*

In 2007, I got a full time job, working evenings and weekends, so I didn't spend near as much time with Robert and Crystal as I had in the years prior. For the most part, I have always had a relationship with them.

In 2013 when I told Robert that I had been attending at Life.Church, he was understanding, but not really accepting of what I was doing. I really think that he was just nervous for me because he didn't know anything about Life.Church, or about the people I was spending so much time with. For a little while, it was a little awkward around Robert and Crystal because I knew that they were trying to understand where I was coming from. At that time, they were still involved in the assembly, so it put us at different places, but I never doubted that Robert was there for me, like he had always been.

Since that time, Robert and Crystal have also left the assembly and have been on a faith filled journey of their own.

I have been so excited to see what God is doing with their lives, and it makes me so happy to see the joy and freedom they have in Christ.

I wasn't ever really close to Crystal, but in the last year or so, I feel like Crystal has become one of my closest friends. She has been there for me through so many bumps along the way. I love that I can call her at any given moment and know that she is there with encouragement and wisdom.

Robert and Crystal have been my biggest cheerleaders while writing this book, constantly encouraging me and pushing me to keep going.

*~I could not have gotten through this book without you both and I love you more than I can tell you. Thank you for all of the love and support that you have given me. I am so thankful for your part in my life, and I am so excited to see where your own journey takes you.*

Jessica – I met Jessica in May of 2013, and my life has never quite been the same since.

I am an introvert, and I have never been really comfortable with physical contact. When Jessica gave me like three hugs the first afternoon I met her, I was sure that we were never going to get along very well.

I met Jessica on Sunday afternoon when she walked me through the LifeKids orientation. Then we ended up having a special conversation, in which she told me that when I was ready to tell my family about attending Life.Church, to let her know because she wanted to pray over me before I told them. I did not even know how to respond to that. No one, in my entire life of being in a Christian environment, had ever said something like that to me before. It really touched my heart, and I will never forget it. A few weeks later, when I was ready to talk to my family, I told Jessica. She got a few leaders together, and they prayed over me.

Over the couple years that I have known Jessica, there have been so many times that she has prayed over me, or sat in the "log" (a hallway in LifeKids that is decorated like a log) and encouraged me, or just let me talk about what was going on in my world.

Jessica was the first one that really encouraged me to put my story on paper and I really balked at the idea for a long time. Finally God helped me see that I should be writing this book. Jessica has been right by my side the whole way, cheering me along, and even helping me figure out a title.

Jessica also gave me my very first Christmas eve, complete with leaving cookies and milk for Santa, feeding the reindeer, watching Christmas movies while we wrapped presents late at night because we had been at church all day, and then waking up early to open the presents in our pjs.

~ *I will never forget the way you welcomed me into your life when I was so new at serving in LifeKids, and I treasure all of the crazy moments we had serving together. I love you, my polar opposite friend!*

Justin and Stormie – I really don't even know where to begin to tell you about these dear friends.

I met Justin in July of 2007 when I started my job at the bank. He also worked there, although he was in a different department than I was. I was actually scared of him for several years, although I am really not sure why! Finally, I realized that he wasn't that scary, and we started chatting a little more, here and there, at work and soon became friends.

There have been countless times that Justin has let me talk things out, and he always makes so much more sense of things, often challenging me with questions that make me think deeper.

I met Stormie, Justin's wife, at a work function in December of 2013, and she has been such a huge blessing in my life ever since.

There have been so many times that Justin and Stormie have welcomed me into their home as part of their family, including giving me my very first Christmas day.

It was December of 2013, and I had spent Christmas Eve at Jessica's house. I was invited to Justin and Stormie's house for Christmas day dinner. When I arrived, I was a little nervous because I hadn't realized that all of Justin's family was going to be there, but I was completely welcomed with open arms. I was so overwhelmed with how everyone was so glad that I was there, even though they didn't know me. It was a very special time for me.

Since then, I have been welcomed into many of their family gatherings, and I sincerely feel like a part of their family.

*"It is so hard to understand how these people, who barely know me, care more about me than my own family does. It doesn't even make sense."* -journal entry May 14, 2013

Justin and Stormie have been there for me so many times during the few years that I have known them, both work related, and in my personal life. *~Anna Banana here, you both mean so much to me. Thank you for all of the wisdom and encouragement that you poured into me. I will never forget the hours that we have sat on the back porch talking, the random little chats during the week, singing at Waterloo, swimming during the summer, the red blanket that is waiting for me any time that I invite myself over (especially any time there is bad weather), or the refrigerator rights. I love you both!*

## My Tuesday Night Girls
- Six of us girls have been going to dinner every other Tuesday night since February of 2014, and it has been so much fun. I have so many special memories of our Tuesday nights. Reading a book together, Christmas gift exchange, celebrity crushes, my first trip to Bricktown (including, but not limited to, jay walking), broken hearts, All The Single Ladies, two out of the six of us getting married, hashing out details after one of us would go on a date, movie nights watching "Best of Me" and discussing Scott Eastwood, and so many more fun memories. I could fill an entire book of all the memories, all the fun places we have eaten, and all the crazy conversations we have had.

When I first decided to write this book, I told the girls at Tuesday night dinner, while we were sitting in Urban Johnnies. I was waiting for them to bring me a new piece of salmon because they had brought the first piece out raw. I was a little nervous telling them about my book, but as soon as I said what I wanted to do, they all jumped behind me 100%. It means so much to me. One of the girls told me they get the first five copies once it is in print.

*~ Each of you girls are so special to me, and I am so thankful that God placed you in*

*my life. There are a lot of different personalities within our little group, but each of you are so awesome in your own way. Thank you so much for the part that each of you have in my life. Love you ladies!*

# Spiritual Ninjas - One Sunday afternoon in October of 2013, I was
sitting in the office at Life.Church talking with Jessica, and a guy walked in
and started talking to her. Jessica then introduced this guy, Ryan, to me and
told me that he was a LifeGroup leader and that I should really think about
going to his LifeGroup. She had been encouraging me for some time to get
plugged into a LifeGroup, but for the last year, I had been in so many new
places and met new people, and I just wasn't ready to be the "new person"
again quite yet.

I talked to Ryan for a few minutes, and we exchanged numbers, and I told
him that I promised I would come one time and see what it was about, but
I did not make any promises past that.

The first week that I went to LifeGroup, it was a fun and fellowship night.
We all went to dinner at Hideaway. There were about 20 people there that
night and I was completely overwhelmed. I didn't know anyone except
Ryan, and I had only met him briefly a week or so before. It was all I could
do to make it through dinner, and then I headed home, knowing that I
wouldn't be going back.

At that time, I was still very quiet and reserved, and I felt like an idiot
showing up in my jean skirt and long hair. I knew that everyone else
probably thought I was crazy.

I didn't go back to that LifeGroup for several weeks. Each Sunday
morning, I would see Ryan in LifeKids, and he would encourage me to
come back, but I managed to push him off for some reason or another. I
knew that I could not handle that many extroverts every single Monday
night.

Ryan finally wore me down, and I agreed to come back and give the group
another chance.

I went back to the LifeGroup on a normal Monday night, and it was still
overwhelming, but not quite as bad. Although I got lost so I was late and I
was very embarrassed about that, but I was soon made to feel very
welcome.

Over the next two years, the group of people has changed some as some
have gotten married and moved on, and others have joined the group, and
it has had a couple different changes in the leadership, but they are still an
amazing group of people I feel honored and blessed to do life with.

This group of people is there for each other when someone is going
through a loss, a trial, a happy, joyful time, or anything else that life throws
our way.

These people encourage me, teach me (things like never play Quelf with

Ryan!), bless me, and push me to become a better me. This is the family that God has given me, and I wouldn't trade them for all of the blood relatives in the world.

# Meg
- Meg is the best baby sister anyone could ever have. I was 8 years old when Meg was born so it was like I had my own, real live, baby doll. I remember when Meg was born, Dad took Charlotte and I both to Toys 'R' Us and he bought us each a new doll, because "if Mom got a new baby, then we got a new baby, too."

Meg and I got close after Charlotte got married. That left Meg and I the only kids left at home. When I moved out when I was 25, Meg helped me so much, getting the new place ready, and helping me unpack and decorate a house. Then, when I moved in to town a year later, Meg was such a big help again.

There were several times that Meg would come and stay with me at my apartment. We would always stay up late and watch movies and eat Sour Patch Kids.

When Meg got engaged during the summer of 2014, she spent even more time at my apartment, knowing that she would soon be moving to Montana, and we wouldn't get to see each other very often. We were close before that summer, but we got even closer through hours of wedding shopping and planning, and dreaming about what her life was going to be like living so far away.

In December of 2014, I had the blessing of being one of Meg's bridesmaids at her wedding. We had so much fun planning the wedding and making it happen. It was such a fun day, and yes, we were ahead of schedule the entire day. I loved the privilege of being at Meg's side during her special day. It had a couple hard moments because some of our family at the wedding did not approve of the choices that either of us were making, but I felt like it brought us even closer together.

It was very hard for me to see Meg pack up and move so far away and know that I wouldn't get to see her very often. We promised to write each other, and we have done very well at keeping that promise. I love our letters; they are like a conversation that never ends.

*~ I am so thankful for your relationship, and I will treasure it always! Thank you for all of your support as I have been writing this book! Your input means the world to me. I love you, Meglet*

# Heather
- It was a May camp-out, and every year, on the last day, we would have a giant water fight. The summer I was 12 years old, I was in the middle of the water fight when a little brown haired girl about my age grabbed my hand and told me that she knew where some really cold water

was. We ran to her family's camper and got melted ice out of the ice chests to throw on people, and we have been best friends ever since.

There are a lot of people who are never blessed with having a best friend to go through life with, but Heather was that person to me.

She lives in Virginia so over the years we haven't gotten to spend a lot of time together. As we have become adults, we try to get together at least a couple times a year. We didn't see each other much when we were younger so we wrote letters to each other to keep in touch.

Through the years we have gone through so much together, and there was a period of about four years that we didn't speak to each other at all because of being at different places in our lives. Yet, when the time was right, God brought us back together again.

We started talking to each other again in the winter of 2012, and we have just gotten closer and closer since then.

I have so many special memories of my times with Heather, including building a human pyramid going down the road in a travel trailer, picking thorns off all of the roses for Crystal's wedding, sleeping sideways in your bed, staying up way too late talking about boys, going snipe hunting, all the times we have surprised each other (including the time you jumped out of the trunk at me!), coffee at Joe's, having our hearts broken, Catfish and Pebbles, rock climbing at Robber's Cave, painting the horses hooves, and so many more memories.

*~ Heather, I am so thankful that God placed you in my life all those years ago. You have been such an encouragement to me and have been such a great support to me while I have been writing this book. Love you!*

There are others that I must thank for all the help they have given me with this book:

**Valerie Danels**- Thank you for all your hard work spell checking and proof reading my manuscript and letting me email you with a hundred other questions. Your help and encouragement has been a huge blessing!

**Kim Kimberling**- Thank you for your advice and input, and for writing the wonderful foreword for my book. It means so much that you would invest in me this way. I will never forget the advice you shared with me the first time we met: "If you are being called to write this book, never let anything anyone tells you, keep you from writing it".

**Caleb and Hannah Collins**- Thank you for the wonderful photo shoot. Not only are the photos perfect, I had a really good time working with you both.

There are so many others who have been cheering me on as I have been working on this book. Thank you so much for all of the support.

You'll Never Be Loved

Anna Stamper

You'll Never Be Loved

Anna Stamper

Made in the USA
Charleston, SC
26 March 2016